A Diary of a Roller-Coaster Ride:

In Between
Euphoria
and
Melancholy

Safira Mardjono

For book orders, email orders@traffordpublishing.com.sg

Most Trafford Singapore titles are also available at major online book retailers.

Printed in Singapore.

ISBN: 978-1-4669-9126-2 (sc)
ISBN: 978-1-4669-9127-9 (hc)
ISBN: 978-1-4669-9128-6 (e)

Trafford rev. 04/26/2013

T**ff**ForD www.traffordpublishing.com.sg

Singapore
toll-free: 800 101 2656 (Singapore)
Fax: 800 101 2656 (Singapore)

To Mama.

INTRODUCTION

If you met my mother, I think you would like her. Most people describe her as funny, often naively witty, and energetic. She is also driven and knows her priorities. She gets things done—I don't know how—and is one of the hardest working people I know. She was on scholarships all the way through her PhD in pharmacy. At a glance, she would strike you as Wonder Woman, providing our small family with such luxury and comfort despite being a single mother.

But she is also good at hiding things: the divorce, her tears, her weakness at handling my highs and lows. We had our fights when plates would break and our cats would run away from our screaming and crying. But she is the best mother and caretaker I could ask for.

My father was a quiet man who loved his hobbies. I remember one of them being golf. We had so many trophies from all his golf competitions he won. I don't know where they are now. I think they just got lost during (the far too often) house movings. He would tell me stories, but I forgot what kinds. He loved antique stores and culture. He never shared much; I never asked much. But we loved food, and sometimes he would ask questions.

But I resented him. When I was on puberty, I resented him. I resented him because my mother was the sole breadwinner, and he was always at home doing nothing. I started ignoring what he had to say and would never answer his questions. Finally, all of us just drifted away and didn't live in the same house anymore.

I loved my father. I just think we were so similar in a way that we didn't know how to express certain things, and so we just kept quiet about them. I bet if he were still here, we would be having conversations and find that we have so much in common.

Primary school was rough, junior high was OK, and high school was smooth . . . and clean. I wasn't crazy in high school—not at all. I think if I had to choose the best version of me in my life, the most stable, clean version of me, I would choose me in high school.

And that was when and where I met you. You have always been and will always be one of the most significant people in my life. Even if it's not the same anymore, and if we one day have our own families, maybe I will tell my children about youth and about you—how youth can be spent without drugs and alcohol yet can still be very fulfilling and memorable.

I wouldn't lie, and I am not afraid to write any of these things.

But after you, relationships became harder and harder to sustain. I became weaker, more vulnerable, and far too open to all of the wrong things. I think, instead of making friends, I started making enemies instead. I am constantly at war with myself, with doctors, medications, and death.

In the second year of college, I realised that something was wrong. For some period of time, I stopped going to my classes altogether and just lost interest in all kinds of activities. For days I stayed in my room, blinds closed, with only one night lamp on. I slept all day and cried all night. I saw no point in living, despite going to the best university in the country and getting almost straight A's. No, I saw no point in all of that. I never felt more alone in my life; I was helpless, and everything seemed bleak. The proximity of death was inexplicable.

When I finally decided to go to classes, something happened. It was as if my blood in every vein in my body was sucked down into the earth by heavy gravity, and I would start losing my breath. I would fall down on to the floor and would lie down there for at least a few minutes, then stand up again only to wonder where the hell I was—when in fact, I hadn't left my room for days. I was lost. I had no idea what was happening. Later on, I found out that it was derealisation caused by repeated panic attacks.

When things started to feel better, and blinds were finally opened, I decided to see a GP. She listened but didn't speak a word, and then she prescribed me antidepressants, which later resulted in the worst mania I have ever experienced in my life. Just two days after I started taking them, I was enraged. I had all this energy, but I was so angry. It was just plain rage. I didn't know what I was raging about, or what or whom was I so mad at. I started throwing things, including phones, plates—just everything in sight. Instinctively, I stopped taking the medication and swore that I would never see any GP again. But later on, I realised that she only saw the depression, and it was not her fault because I hadn't experienced my mania until a few weeks later when I was on my break in Jakarta.

In Jakarta, I had nothing to do, yet I had all this energy that I just had to channel. I needed some kind of stimulation. I started going out more, and not long after, I self-medicated. Parties were great; I made a lot of friends. For most days, I was happy. I loved Jakarta; it never felt more like home. My self-confidence was over the top. Holiday flings felt fulfilling, though I knew I was never in love with any of them. In short, life had never felt better, and that was the best holiday feeling I could recall.

Until one day, my energy level was still high. I threw plates against the wall. I was frustrated; I didn't know what to do. I was so angry with everything; I felt it raging inside me. I started crying and shouting. Out of frustration, I took a knife from the kitchen drawer, and that moment became my first attempt. Then one my cats approached me and lay down on top of my feet. Then I saw my mother standing not very far from where I was standing. She didn't speak a word; tears were running down her face, and her gaze was fixed. Then she asked me, "What do you want? You want to die? Is that what you want?" I realised then I needed help. I didn't really want to die, but I didn't know how else to stop feeling what I was feeling.

That was when the journey began. The journey of cocktails of medications, which resulted in weight gain, failed relationships, harsh social consequences, bad reputation—betrayal by the people whom I considered friends due to my addiction, misunderstandings, and so on. To date, I am still struggling with it, and I don't think I have come to terms with it. But I'm trying my best. I haven't given up just yet.

I have made very bad decisions, and I am constantly asking whether my leaps of judgement were biological in nature or if they were just a matter of make-believe. The social consequences were hard. Sometimes, I would meet people who understood, who understood what it feels like to be misunderstood, who have the condition or dealt with a person with that condition. I thank God I met them. I thank God that in the midst of all this madness, sanity is indeed relative and that I am not the only person who is at war, because everybody is fighting his or her own battle.

But you always understand. During my "closet" moments, miles away, you would always pick up my call. During my most vulnerable moments, you were always there and said all the right things, even if I didn't want to hear them. It's because of people like you, like Mom, like the best friends I've made, that I held back the urge to end it all, again and again.

Sometimes, I wonder if I will survive long enough to have a family of my own. As I said, the proximity of death can be inexplicable. I can still recall the attempts I have made, although I don't expect you to understand my state of mind at the time: the bleakness, the feeling of helplessness, the disappointment—basically just all the sadness bottled up into one moment. Many have died from bipolar disorder, but I am thrilled to not become one of its victims.

July 22, 2009

Energy?

When I went to my science lecture today, the lecturer told us an interesting fact that I never knew: no one has ever been able to describe what energy is. I mean, have you ever thought about that? Energy is everywhere; it's around us. Hell, we *are* energy—flesh and bones made up from particles of energy. I know it can be transformed from one form to another, but where does it come from?

Maybe sometimes human beings are just not able to explain everything. Can they explain the reason for their existence? Though the definition of *explain* might be a bit blurry, it is still a quite puzzling fact. As an agnostic, I still find it kind of hard to accept the fact that there *might* be something bigger, something more powerful than all human beings gathered together. Others may call it God. Has anyone ever explained what God is? Well, maybe in the Koran or the Bible someone might've described what God is like, but where did God come from? How? No one knows. I guess that might be the reason I'm still struggling to believe in God; there is just not enough explanation.

But maybe sometimes you don't need an explanation, just like energy. You know what it's like and what it does, and you know that it *does* exist. And maybe that's enough. Maybe we aren't yet capable of explaining everything. I believe in energy; I know it exists. Maybe God exists too.

October 13, 2009

Paradox

Why do we change? Do we really change, or is it just our self-mechanism talking in order to adapt to new situations? Is there a core trait that exists within each of us that never changes over time and across situations? Our implicit attitude, perhaps?

Why do *we* change? How did things become the way they are now? Things were good; *we* were good. I wish I understood what happened, or is it the real us talking here? Are we no longer hidden behind our masks? Was I never aware of a mask I had put on before?

Who are we?

I've always said to myself that I should stay true to myself, but sometimes I'm not sure which part of myself I should hold on to. I always feel like I'm a mixture of different selves, but they are all *me.* Yet they often contradict each other. I can be all warm, affectionate, and friendly, but at times, I am cold, bitter, and indifferent.

And I'm sorry if I ever hurt *you.*

October 19, 2009

Heartless?

Someone said I don't have a heart. Do I? Why do I often wish I *didn't?* I wish I could construct my own emotions or start all over again, free from any premises and ideas. Is there really something that is pure and innocent deep inside all of us, untouched by the society we live in?

Or there is no heart and there never was. A heart is a means of controlling the world—ruling you by your own emotions that you often think you have no control over. Do we have control over such things? Can we erase everything that is written in the book and just write nothing? Is it ever possible?

October 29, 2009

Home

What is home? What makes a place, or a setting, feel like home? Is it the place or the people, per se, or is it the combination of both? To what extent does each matter?

What good is a place when you've got no one to enjoy it with?

Can the most unpleasant place turn into heaven when you're with the right people?

I'm currently contemplating my own concept of "home." When I think of the word *home*, the first image that pops out in my mind is the people I love at this place I love. What a soothing feeling that thought gives me. I guess it's the combination of both indeed.

November 2, 2009

Is it possible not to share the same perception of reality? I mean, what if we don't assume that we share the same basic "knowledge"? Is it possible not to assume?

Emotions are said to be socially constructed, and to be able to manage our emotions completely makes us seem like robots. How do we know when we reach a state in which our heart is overly managed? Is an overly managed heart a sign of inhumanity? Does being able to manage our emotions mean we are independent of our own emotions? Or does it mean that we are in touch with ourselves, completely accepting emotions as part of ourselves? Are we fools to be controlled by our undermanaged heart, our own emotions? Is there a point where everything is balanced? What is it to be balanced?

November 13, 2009

Heaven?

What is death? Is death merely an ending of life or a start of another whole new thing? Is life never-ending? I've always thought that after we die, we just . . . die. I was never scared of hell or the suffering that we all supposedly—according to the religious—have to endure. I don't think I can ever believe any of that. Maybe I am just too arrogant, or naive, to believe that we are created only to experience pleasure and to be tortured later on. Isn't God supposed to be the absolute symbol of *unconditional* love?

What happens when we die? Does the soul exist? There are a number of kinds of heavens that I have read of (all of which are fictional, obviously), but I like the concept of a heaven where everything in my life is explained to me. It's like the one in *The Five People You Meet in Heaven*, although I'm not really sure if it was meant to be heaven or just a transition to wherever he was going or something. But yes, isn't it better than the concept where you get everything you want *forever*? Even the word *forever* frightens me; it seems so long—too long. If we were to get whatever we wanted, wouldn't it be boring and ordinary? Would I be able to ask to just stop or go back to living? Or does boredom not exist in heaven?

Maybe it will be different for each of us. I'd like to think that it would be the happiest place, with everything explained, but then there would be no mystery left. Maybe heaven is just contentment, or maybe it is a state of mind, or being, in which you feel peaceful and content.

November 17, 2009

<u>0</u>

Since when have balloons become accessories of a party? I don't like balloons; they are fragile and passive.

What is it about denial that makes it so tempting to hold on to? I thought I had dealt with the fact that life changes, but it turns out I really haven't. It's like a balloon—I can pick the colour, and its presence makes life like a party. But, you see, a balloon is still just a balloon; it's fragile, and the only things that make it up are air and a tiny, delicate layer of elastic rubber. Too much pressure or heat can pop it; no matter how strong it looks or how hard it tries to act as a jacket around the air inside, it can blow.

How strong are we, really? What holds us together? Our values, culture, or people (or, more specifically, the people we love and care about)? Do they all interrelate to each other? One thing can lead to another; when one breaks, it can break us apart.

I miss my safety net, my glue that holds all my pieces together.

December 1, 2009

If Life Were a Maze

When you look at the big picture, everything seems so simple, so easy. There is *always* a way out. But when you are in that big picture, it feels *big*. You get lost and confused, and everything seems so complicated, especially when dealing with all the fabric details. When you're not in the labyrinth, it's easier to find *the* way out, but when you are in it, it becomes *your* way out. You become part of the labyrinth; it involves you and impacts you, and what you do has consequences that have to do with you.

Emotional attachment is often the hardest; it blurs your vision, clouds your judgement. Sometimes, it's hard to tell whether it's a distortion or something that matters. You see, I often wish I were heartless, because then everything would be much easier—no heartaches, pain, or bad feelings as consequences. But is it really the answer to be a robot? What is life without feelings, without love?

Is detaching yourself the best way to look at things differently and see the big picture? What if you *do* know the answer but you just can't? If life were a maze, would it be the kind that you just have to go through, occasionally finding things along your way, or the never-ending kind? Or maybe the kind where you get something in the end—but when is the end? I don't think you'll ever know. And to think that we are here to be granted something someday after having gone through everything just sounds too naive for me. Is life an achievement?

Maybe life isn't anything to be solved—just enjoy the wild ride, perhaps?

April 22, 2010

<u>o</u>

Others define us.

You might not agree with me at this point; perhaps you never will. Well, what I mean is—again throwing out a question I do not intend to answer—how are we defined? Are we defined by our relationships with others? What kinds of relationships? Or are we defined by how we treat other people, or how we treat *ourselves*?

How different can you be when you're alone, when there is no one to communicate with other than yourself? Are we defined by how we communicate? How do we define ourselves when the only mirror is our own perception?

Or perhaps I am just again dwelling on a pointless matter?

May 5, 2010

Denial

Do you believe in denial?

How can one deny something so obvious, like death? Perhaps denial disguises itself in a more subtle form, such as the "existence" of the afterlife. Is the truth too painful to handle? The thought of something just gone forever is too upsetting, perhaps. So many afterlife concepts, so many forms of denial.

Oh, well. I guess people cope in different ways. Anything to keep us sane is OK, I guess. But then, what is it to be sane?

Personally for me, and I don't care if you judge me or whatever, I don't really "talk" to my dad, or God, or any unseen being. But again, maybe that's just my way of coping. Talking to something that's not there (your definition of what is "there" might be different from mine) just feels simply ridiculous. I guess when I mourn, I go nostalgic and wonder what I could have, and should, have done, and that makes me feel even worse. I accept the fact that people die, but I don't really believe in the afterlife.

They're gone, buddy. I can deal with, "They live in your heart," but other than that . . . Hmm, call me close minded.

Am I in denial? Who knows?

May 7, 2010

∴

Tuhan itu tidak ada.
Tuhan itu ada.

apa maksudnya ada? apa kata tuhan bisa mewakili Tuhan? Tuhan itu apa sih?

siapa? apa? siapa? apa? kenapa?

June 12, 2010

<u>**Concepts. Ideas**</u>

Everything is a concept. How we see our lives, how we live, how things should be, they're all based on concepts. We're learning about concepts every day, pursuing this and that degree, just to learn more concepts later on. We get paid by the concept of money, just to trade it with the concept of fun and survival. What is it to survive? All these scholars are arguing about concepts, talking to each other in journals, which then need to be verified according to certain rules and concepts.

I'm sick of concepts.

Now that I've repeated the word so many times, it feels strange. Concept. You need to be able to master the conceptual thinking if you want to ace school.

I wonder why beggars seem so deluded yet happy. Well maybe not all of them, but you know the kind.

I seriously doubt the idea of living life to the fullest. How do you live your life to the *fullest*? Is it achieving? Learning more concepts? Exploring? Life is all there is. If there's an idea I agree with, it's probably just, "Seize the day." *Carpe diem.*

Maybe God itself is a concept. Almost four years ago, I said to my teacher that perhaps God exists because we think that he *does* exist. In other words, *we* create his existence. Until now, I have no proof that he does. Perhaps I haven't yet found the proof because I have no faith in his existence in the first place. I need to be open to the idea first, but then it goes around in a circle. But then again it's faith—believing something without sufficient evidence. So I guess it indeed is a matter of wanting to believe.

Are we not happy with what it is that we need to complicate things?

July 5, 2010

I hate when people categorize. We are human beings. Categories are made by us for others. How do you know what to know? If beauty is in the eye of the beholder, then we all have different eyes, don't we?

July 16, 2010

?

What does it mean to be rational? Or irrational? If logic is said to be rational but logic itself was made by humans to explain things in their own terms, what if terms don't help? Explaining things in terms of other things, answering things by throwing out another question that questions the previous question. Ha ha ha. This is a never-ending cycle, isn't it?

Why?

Because it is just what it is. Why do we always feel the need to have things explained? I just want contentment—that's all. No questioning, no doubting, just accepting. But then there is a thin line between accepting and being blind (folded). And I can't fool myself by pretending not to care.

July 19, 2010

At times like these, some faith would be useful, but what kind? A faith that there is a being that controls everything in the universe? That it will take care of everything? That everything is going to be just *fine*?

Or a faith that I will go through this anyways? It's just a phase, and this too will pass. A faith that these feelings will go away. All this guilt, resentment, and nostalgia. The fear. I'm so scared to go back, scared of the feelings I know I will have to face, the loneliness, the panic attacks, and the anger.

But of course, there are always two sides of everything. You know, see it from another point of view. The positive side. Wait. Are we just looking for reasons to justify things? A denial to make ourselves feel better?

July 25, 2010

<u>Place, Home, Mobility?</u>

So in a way, movement occurs to resolve an imbalance, always for a reason. But when it seems like there's no reason, does it mean that do we just not know it yet?

How can society, culture, people, and the way we live be analyzed by natural science? Science. Social science. Again, how can we explain things in terms of other things?

Movement as a means to an end. And another branch of thinking emerged, as David said, called *humanism*, that puts humans into analyses. Feelings, emotions, bodies . . . Relationships between people and places.

Place, not merely as somewhere to live, has become some kind of centre of everything, as a fundamental human need. Attachment to the place. "Mobile people often do not develop this kind of attachment to places." (Mom, this reminds me of you. The mobile woman, ha ha.) Mobility erodes this kind of capability to develop attachment with a place? Sounds very negatively imploded.

Space can be seen as a means of controlling people, putting people into these boxes of space.

Sense of belonging, identity . . . movement, mobility. The concept of "home."

July 26, 2010

"Things happen for a reason," but what would you do when you can't justify the things that happen(ed) by any means? Or should you stop looking for reasons and just *accept* it? Because it is what it is.

But accepting seems pretty hard.

kita pikir kita adalah kita,
kita atau saya?
saya atau kita?
berkaca dari mata orang lain,
apakah mata sendiri mengutarakan kebenaran?
menurut siapa?

dibentuk dari abu-abu terbang, kata orang kotor
emang mereka udah mandi?
memandikan diri dari apa?
mereka bilang saya kotor, tapi
semua cuma perkiraan masing-masing
semua benar, semua salah

memasukkan diri sendiri ke tembok-tembok buatan
berharap itu memberikan penjelasan atas apa
bohong, ini cuma kosong
kenapa tidak puas dengan kekosongan? ketelanjangan?

August 1, 2010

If you haven't been wrong, or at least been accused that you were, how would you be able to differentiate right and wrong? How can you be sure if A really is A if you haven't seen anything other than A?

August 4, 2010

Temperamental, emotional—sometimes too emotional. I feel emotions too deeply. I'm too excited or too angry, too nostalgic or too "seizing the day." Confused. I'm confused. What else is there to know?

August 10, 2010

<u>Homesick</u>

I'm so homesick it's not funny. I miss everything about home. Lying in bed for hours, not having to do anything all day. Going out with my loves to the places I love. Laughing like crazy until my eyes get wet. Doing something so random and useless all day. Nothing has to be planned; everything just goes as it is.

I miss cuddling with my cats. I miss being woken up by the purr of them with my inhaler next to my pillow because of their fur. I miss Mbak Asih, the only maid who actually cares, along than others, of course.

I miss driving. I miss getting lost alone. I miss the crowd, the traffic. I miss having lunch at this place, dinner at this place, and so on.

I miss random convos where every word just flows naturally. No matter how random, we know nothing needs to be understood. I miss the deep talks, questioning why the world is the way it is . . . and end up with no concrete answers.

August 18, 2010

:

I suck at maintaining—maintaining grades, health, life (how do you maintain *this*?), relationships—both intimate and casual—emotions, goals, peace, money . . .

I know that nothing stays the same, but I would like some longer periods of constancy, please! But of course, not when things are on the shitty ends, ha ha. I mean, in terms of academic achievement, I'm always all fired up at the beginning, very determined, head is full of big ideas . . . and then here comes the results. I'm satisfied, too comfortable, too relaxed.

Relationships—the honeymoon phase. Everything is good, wonderful. Compromise is beyond questioning. The true selves come out, stubborn beyond compromise—selfish, withdrawn, too attached, detached? Do I have issues with commitment? I don't know.

August 19, 2010

Utopia is *always* just around the corner. We need progress and advancement in this and that to achieve this particular state of life, but are we ever satisfied? It seems to me like we're climbing a never-ending ladder—some people optimistically—hoping to achieve something by the end of the ladder. And some with the couldn't-care-less attitude.

Does the concept change as we progress?

August 21, 2010

Admitting the "truth" to yourself might sometimes be the hardest thing to do. Sometimes, I found myself trying to justify things—but only you know the answer, the truth. The truth is I would like to believe in the existence of God, and I'm tired of seeking evidence. I believe because I want to believe, and that, I guess, is what faith is. I can believe that Santa Claus does exist just for the sake of child-like excitement when Christmas comes. (This wouldn't be entirely true since I don't celebrate Christmas, but it's an example.) I need to believe there is something greater, just for the sake of the comfort that lies behind faith. Security, hope, I'm tired of always being too cynical.

In terms of the "truth," there is no such thing as truth. The truth here is the feeling that is often ignored, suppressed, forgotten. I was mad. I didn't want to admit it. I was disappointed, isolated, hurt—you name it. Why are we so afraid of experiencing *fully* every emotion there is? Why do we need to justify things in order to feel right? To not feel certain ways? I'm not saying that we should drown in a pool of emotions, but accepting . . . It isn't easy, but the more we run, the more we fall in too deep. It's like digging our own graves without realising that we are.

September 2, 2010

Spreading both wings, left and right. What about the other life? The other life you've had all your life. How can you switch from A to B in a matter of hours? Neither here or there, neither dead or alive.

September 3, 2010

Privacy is the only thing an individual can have. What is privacy? Is it merely an idea of enjoying solitude? Personal space? What is personal space? Every time I lost my BlackBerry, I secretly wished it would just be gone so I wouldn't have to deal with having to reply to messages and all the pings! It's good when you're bored and when communication *is* necessary. I just wish we weren't so accessible. It almost feels like I have no personal space, even when I'm alone.

It was so much easier when texts just meant texts, not messengers (and this alone can refer to so many types of messenger) or any other kinds of text-involving applications. It was so much simpler when you didn't know and didn't have to let the other know whether the message had been read or not. It's all become so specific, so invading. Why would you mind if your message has been read and they don't reply? Speculations, rejection? Seriously, life was so much simpler before BlackBerry.

If this is the kind of progress we are looking at, I would rather go backwards.

September 6, 2010

To be honest, my favourite feeling in the world is gloomy. I only feel at my best when it's all gloomy—it makes everything seem so honest, so real. It brings tranquillity and peacefulness. I don't get how some people just can't stand gloominess because it's "too depressing." The world isn't only about happy faces, and the fast pace of mobility can be so overwhelming. Some people prefer a getaway to the sun, to the beach. I prefer somewhere crowded and empty at the same time, beautiful, and gloomy.

Of course, everyone has his or her own definition of what is beautiful, and a place can't be judged generally. There are particular spots in some cities that make my heart pound so hard it makes existence feel so real, while at the same time it brings peacefulness. And the rest. The rest of the city can be so ordinary and colourless.

Crowded and empty at the same time, with dimmed city lights.

September 14, 2010

Have you ever felt like you're in an alien world? Not the kind of UFO alien or like you're stranded on Mars or something, but your surrounding just doesn't fit. Reality seems unreal. Sometimes, I need to give myself a mild slap in the face to make sure that this *is* real. Sometimes, I even get so unsure about myself, who I am, and why I am here, not in a philosophical way but physically why and who. When people talk to me, I can seem so absent-minded because I would be thinking to myself about that very moment. Why? I never cease to understand.

I'm scared that I might be going insane. What if someday I really do snap and won't come back? That kind of "unreal" feeling and the intense déjà vu usually occur as the first stage of a panic attack, though I haven't had them lately. Some people told me to try to go off Lamictal, but what if I really do have bipolar disorder or whatever? What if it really does help with the fucked-up episodes and the panic attacks? I really don't know where I should draw the line between the pros and cons. Is it the cause or the side effect? What the hell is wrong?

September 16, 2010

It's the neurotic who gets things done, but she gets so stressed to the point that she can't cope. So the cold-headed takes over and everything is stable again, normal again, but there is no sense of pressure to get moving. She just wants to gaze at the clouds and not move. The neurotic is knocking from the inside to tell her that time is running fast and they're getting left behind, but she replies that she needs to take it slowly, to breathe. This is too slow. We're not moving.

September 20, 2010

My dad liked fish. I'm not sure if fish was his favourite dish, but he liked to keep fish as pets and he liked to fish every once in a while. I didn't get why my fish, in my tank I cared by myself, always died while his didn't. Of course, he had the big one inside the house, with all the lights and the cool fish and all. I've always thought fishing was boring, and I didn't get why he could sit for hours waiting for a fish to take the bait. I didn't get so many things. Maybe it would be different now. The difference is that I'm just going to try those things and grasp the feel of it on my own.

September 26, 2010

When I was taking a walk down by the lake, I noticed there were two kids playing with sands. There were burying their hands in the sands, circling their fingers, and they seemed so content. I remember when I was a kid I found joy in playing with sand. It was nice. I didn't have enough past to remember by yet, and no future to think about. I was living in the present moment, and that present moment was how the sand felt when it rubbed against my finger skin. I was amazed by the fact that no matter how hard I tried to make the ground appear smooth, the space between my fingers always left traces on the sand.

September 27, 2010

I am sorry for being judgemental and harsh on you. I am sorry for not knowing what you've been through. I am sorry for leaving things hanging. I am sorry for not saying sorry. I am sorry for letting my huge ego transcend beyond what we had. I am sorry for being a horrible friend I was. I miss you more than I thought I would. I need you; I can't get through this alone.

And I have been trying to find out what's been missing, why this empty hole exists. Maybe it's you. It's the friend I've known for almost seven years now.

September 29, 2010

What's wrong with lying if no one is hurt by it—no one but yourself? I need to stop throwing things away as I'm getting a bit scared of myself. But things are falling into place, or are they? How can you tell? How can I ever know anything? What if something, or someday everything, just falls apart and I spend my time left worrying about how it's going to be?

I love going out alone and sometimes talk to strangers I meet. I guess because you know that there is very little chance that you would see them again, it makes you feel more secure. I sometimes tell my darkest, deepest secrets to strangers I meet. The truth just came out, but I felt like writing it on to a paper and just throwing it away to the ocean and never seeing it again. It's a strange thing, having relationships with people. I take some people for granted because I know they would never leave, but I'm afraid to fully open up because I'm scared that they might leave.

<u>Self-Justifying Tendency</u>

We ascribe meanings to every single thing we encounter, and that's what cognition is all about. But what comes first? Effect or perception? Do we feel what we feel because it just comes naturally to feel that way? Can we control our own feelings? Does justifying really work, or is it merely a form of deception? How far are we willing to go for resolving our cognitive dissonance?

If we all have different ways of perceiving reality, then can I ever really be sure of whether or not I am deceiving myself? Do we tend to stick to those whose perceptions are similar to ours, to justify the way we feel—that we are not alone, not the only one to feel this way? Now that I think about it, it makes everything seem so hollow, so empty, and so meaningless. If meanings are self-constructed, although conditionings are of course inevitable, is there such thing as authenticity then?

Hence, why the self-defence mechanism?

September 30, 2010

There's a void and I can't explain why it's there. Just plain empty. So what are we doing here in life? Working, playing, loving, finding solace in the endless, pointless partying, meeting people, and making impressions on people who don't even matter—and probably never will. How are our attempts in trying to fill up the hole we never knew existed, finding ourselves in one pair of arms after another? Is it false security that we're getting? Is it all that's left of life? To work all your life to make money and to spend it on things that are superficial in nature, to sustain our lives? Are we merely trying to sustain?

What is it that makes life suddenly so unfulfilling, so bleak? What is it about life that makes me feel like despair is all I find in everything I encounter? Why is it that I feel like I'm at the bottom and trying to climb an endless ladder, not even knowing why I keep on climbing? And all this only for the sake of knowing that staying still equals to death?

Why do we try so hard to find love and later despise it because it's unfulfilling? But even after despising it, we later regain our strength and in a false, desperate hope, we find ourselves in love again? How is it that, sometimes, for the sake of having it, we fall for a person who doesn't appreciate us? Why is it that sometimes we stay in an unhappy relationship just because we're too scared of being alone? What is it about being alone that sometimes makes it so scary so that we delude ourselves, fool ourselves into making decisions that we know are bad for us, but keep making them anyway because we are scared of the cold, harsh, bleak reality?

How is it that we are so pressured by the saying that after we make ourselves happy first, then everything comes?

October 1, 2010

I think sometimes it gets to the point where you just don't know what it is, but it has effects on you. It's there. Whatever you do, it's there waiting for you to come back.

October 13, 2010

I've never dreamed of you, not even once. It has been almost six years now. How are you doing up there? It was like we were only biologically related. I forced myself to cry at your funeral, what a cold-hearted bitch I was. And now, years later, I'm starting to understand. It must have been hard being you, being me, being the others. I realised how much I don't know. I thought God was so mean, so harsh, so insensitive, so . . . ungodly.

Please give me a sign. Anything will do, please.

October 14, 2010

And at some point of time, if it exists, everything makes perfect sense—if there's such thing as common sense. My head hurts, but I cannot stop. It's a pure, pure thing. You are here for no reason, because reason is only there to justify. Nothing ever needs to be justified, because conforming is an ugly thing. You are what you are, at the centre of your being. I feel like hugging everyone I meet!

October 16, 2010

What is your fear? Fear lies beyond motivations. Is it the "goal" that we are trying to reach, or is it the thing that we are running from or trying to avoid? Did something happen along the way? Did you stumble? Did you fall? Do stop for a while, see, and listen. See beyond what you explicitly want and understand why you want the things you do now. My little child, stop covering your face with your hands and see.

> Dear Prudence, open up your eyes
> Dear Prudence, see the sunny skies
> The wind is low, the birds will sing
> That you are part of everything
> Dear Prudence, won't you open up your eyes?

October 17, 2010

Why do we need a label? A justification? A reason? A meaning? An acknowledgement? Why should love be labelled as "love"? What makes you so sure that this feeling we all have is perceived the same way? What makes human so self-righteous, so judgemental? I am judgemental, but the more judgement you put on things, the less you are able to see what it truly is. What is? Language is a dangerous weapon. We judge so much and learn so little.

This makes me so sad, so sad to know that to know is dangerous. Knowing makes you powerful and vulnerable at the same time. Sometimes, by knowing you know that you know so little. Powerful when you know, powerless when you know it is just what it is and you can't change it. But why so sad about change? Being sad is like silently watching a tree grow and regretting the fact that it grows; you want some things to stay the same. Why? I think it is only when we stop trying that you can really see. Aren't we all pathetic in some ways? And beautiful, and hopeless, and powerful, and one?

October 18, 2010

L: You are being irrational. You don't make sense.

R: Since when does every single f-ing thing have to make sense? Sense is not common sense. Nobody says you have to conform every single thing you have. Nobody says everything has to be standardized. Sense is what you truly own, what comes with you and what dies with you.

L: But I don't know. Why not be like everyone else? What if they're right? If you don't conform, you will stand alone. How much can you bear? What if all their theories and everything are right? What if right and/or wrong does exist? What if you are making a mistake?

R: Aren't differences beautiful? Do you really want to be just something people implement their ideas onto? To become their ideas? Their way of realising their "ideals"? Their utopia? Why create your own utopia based on others' utopia? Why so vulnerable?

L: I am so confused. So, so confused.

R: You know you always know the answer, because there is no answer.

L: Then what am I looking for? What have I been searching for all this time?

R: You have been trying to fit into others' perceptions.

L: How would you know how and what others perceive? How would you know we are not experiencing the same fucking thing? Why am I so mad? Why do I feel so angry? Why this extremeness?

R: Why keep losing your grip?

L: What grip?

R: You know.

L: No, I don't.

R: The grip isn't external; it's within you. You know that. You've always known that, but sometimes you doubt yourself. So many choices, eh? So many things to choose from.

October 21, 2010

kosong, penuh, kosong, penuh. tanpa ada setengah penuh/kosong apa bedanya kosong dengan penuh?

October 26, 2010

What was mundane to me has changed. Now, mundane is waking up at strange hours, realising that I need to go to a tutorial. I don't always have to wake up at 6.30 and finish everything by two anymore. I now have classes at here and there, scrambled like eggs, although it doesn't make a difference anyway. It's not like I long for those breaks to chat or something, because a break means waiting to resume. Resuming is mundane. Mundane is dragging my body and soul and rushing everything. Mundane is talking to a wall. Mundane is realising that change is needed. Although it's kind of a love and hate affair with life . . . always. I hate and then love everything the next moment. Sometimes, I'm neutral, but I hate being neutral because it makes me feel lifeless, hollow, empty. Then, God, I don't know what I want. But I know I should not listen to myself at *strange hours* . . .

October 27, 2010

Is complexity a trend now? What I dislike:

1. when someone asks me for an opinion he or she doesn't want to hear, and
2. all he or she wants to hear is something to boost the ego.

If you want an ego booster, I will bluntly say that you don't need more.

October 29, 2010

What makes you feel you have the right to "own" other human beings? Possession? What an ugly thing.

October 30, 2010

It's so funny how my life has changed so much in the span of two to three years. A.J., B.J., and Abu are gone, and I can never be really sure whether the rest will still be there when I come home. I still can't believe my mom didn't tell me about their deaths until—what?—four months later? Every time I come back home, there will be another great change, not necessarily good or bad.

Lost a friend, gained a friend. I miss sitting at my old balcony overlooking the Jakarta buildings. I miss the kind of "stability" of my own concept of home. Typical days: alone, cats, Asih comes and goes, bored—three minutes away to PS/Senayan City (and happily waited for Ditit to pick me, up ha ha), home alone and hungry, bakmi japos delivery, and so on . . . And so now, three cats left, and I hate the lighting at the house, though I shouldn't complain . . . *Gh.* And I am now in a city where everything is . . . *Neh,* let's not go there.

Sometimes, I get lost in my own memories and they are like clips that I can relive anytime. But then it means I'm not living in the present, eh? I don't know. The present moment can be so distressing that my memories become a place to resort to. Is it enough to just acknowledge, be grateful, and treasure the best moments? And just like power, (best) memories always comfort and hurt me the most.

Trees grow, eh? I just didn't know that the branches would go to so many different directions . . . Dumbfounded.

October 31, 2010

How can the question "Why?" become such a seemingly important task to work on? A mystery to solve? Do we humans have a need for mysteries? Perhaps if life were so clear and obvious . . . What would we be like? Or perhaps we would just create assumptions, even if they are based on nothing. Thought arises out of nothing. Can something arise out of nothing? I'm not sure which one is the first base here and which one is the last base. Or is it like a circle? No beginning and no end? And inside, we are just trapped inside the circle, trying to figure out what is surrounding us. A tangled web? A maze? Holding hands, faceless? Or do we have different entities surrounding us? Are we part of the thing of someone else's outer lining?

Or are we just alone? What if we all turn out to be schizophrenics? What if everything we see, touch, and feel is not real, built out of our own imagination as something to make up for the loneliness? We are alone and our mind is our only, greatest, and worst companion. What if someday you wake up, alone, in a blank surrounding (or white, if you prefer—it doesn't matter), with no explanation? You try to remember the last place you've gone to before "this," and you just can't remember. You are so convinced about the life you have, but God is playing some sort of trick on you—assuming that it is God that is playing. Perhaps it's to test how much we can rely on our minds or how reliable they are. Can we ever really be sure? I would get a slap from a realist to wake up from rambling like this. This is nonsensical, according to "common" sense, mundane sense.

Oh, I don't know, maybe boredom has become an excuse to escape from this bleakness.

November 8, 2010

But maybe I have a different standard of "stability." My definition of being stable is the process of switching back and forth between being highly energetic and totally immovable. (Read: potato couch.) Maybe I have no neutral ground whatsoever, as I am constantly in-between crying and laughing. I don't get the definition of two-face. People can and do possess contradictive qualities, shown at different times and situations. Why can't some look beyond the layers? Or perhaps to call it a layer wouldn't be entirely appropriate. Sides, maybe? Why not think of it like a cube, or some other 3-D geometrical figure with an unknown number of sides . . . Your call to discover.

November 9, 2010

I hate deaths. I find it really hard to come to terms with the fact that the person will never, ever, come back. I feel stupid talking to something that is not tangible, but if people talk to God, then what's the difference between God and dead people? I've heard about the deaths of so many people lately. Is it sort of like a cycle or something? Is there a time where the numbers just rise up?

A friend of my mom just died last night from cancer. I'd only met him a couple of times, some during business dinners in Jakarta, and I stayed at his house during my stay in Paris in 2005 and 2008. I remember how I loved playing the piano at his house with the cats sitting on the top. He was really French—I'm not sure what the definition of being French really is, but he was just . . . really French. He was smart, stubborn, loving, and he loved wine. He and his wife made this dinner that they called a "special dinner" for me one night. He said I must eat like a Frenchwoman in France. So there were a couple of rounds. I didn't like the appetizer. I thought it was too salty, and believe me: my friends get scared when they see the amount of salt I put into my food. Then there were smoked salmon and cream followed by cheese and crackers. I loved it. He also said, "You're too smart for shopping," which I really hope I can be, if I'm ever too smart for anything. (And my mom always gets freaked out upon seeing my credit card bills.)

My mom said the chemo made him look like a really skinny ninety-year-old—he was sixty. He was big the last time I saw him two years ago. If he knew his life would be ending in two years time, what would he have done? My mom said she couldn't help the tears when she hugged him in August, but he said that he was fine and the cancer was going away. "No need to worry." He even managed to take her to the train station. I was planning to pay him a visit in January, also encouraged by Mom, who was afraid that time might be running out.

He ran out.

I hate deaths. But whatever happens after we die, I hope we are now in a better place, painless. This is what I tell myself every time somebody dies. That I hope that they are in a better place. If there is no place, I just hope that death is a peaceful state and peace will forever remain.

> I told the boy when you dream about bad things happening, it means you're still fighting and you're still alive. It's when you start to dream about good things that you should start to worry. (*The Road*)

I am having relatively good dreams compared to those I had before. I am losing my grip. I have no sense of urgency and motivation at all. I am panicking because I am not panicking yet. Why am I not panicking? I'm letting things slip away. I have no dreams, no goals. Sometimes, I have this wish that I pray before I go to bed, and when I'm sane, it sounds really horrible and I wish I hadn't said it. But when the time comes, it seems logical. It's like in a dream where every stupid thing in real life makes perfect sense.

Perhaps I have been implementing too much neutralizing on myself. I keep convincing myself that everything *is* OK. Maybe I should start telling myself, "No, this is no longer acceptable. This isn't OK." I need to get moving. I need to change this. Perhaps telling ourselves that things are better when they're not is just a denial and makes everything worse. It's like going down the hill and thinking, *It's OK. Nothing bad will happen.* Then boom! You crash. You die. The end. Fin. Ironically, you could have steered your wheel to the left or right where, um . . . Let's just say it's a lot safer than crashing into something in front of you.

Life = me. Me = fluctuating.

Someone, please slap me hard enough to wake me up.

November 10, 2010

Maybe humans do love being told about themselves. Maybe Narcissus is a part of us all, even just a wee bit. Or are we just little insecure beings? Trying to fit in, arranging ourselves to fit in this and that category, thirst for explanations? I know some people who are very, very content, but there is always a price for everything. When you are so content to the point that conforming is no longer necessary, others judge and call you weird. You're weird because you don't wear this particular kind of clothes or because you look like you're from an entirely different galaxy. You're weird because you talk about things that don't "make sense" to most. You're weird because you don't care. You're weird because you don't possess the same kind of understanding of what contentment is. Why?

Isn't it weird how people want to be unique or seen in their own ways, appreciated for their "own" qualities? Do we ever really own anything, even our own "qualities," since everything is socially acquired? I'm not just saying this based on my own superficial daily observations, but this is actually in my psych textbook. People want to be unique, but according to what standards? What criteria? Social expectations are so diverse that fitting in one particular way doesn't mean it's a yes in another. That would be endless . . . Ah, what is contentment?

I know someone who claims to have found inner peace and contentment but ends up preaching about how the world should be perceived and how things really are. It seems so contradictory to me. I mean, if you have come to terms with the fact that differences make one thing and that we are all one, then why keep preaching about your contentment? You even commented on how people behave and pray for them. All right, I'll give you a gold medal for attaining the highest chakra. (I'm not very proud of myself for being this confrontational and judgemental and harsh and all, but . . .) So maybe I'm still lost, maybe I don't see what you see, and maybe someday I will or won't. Maybe I want to, maybe I don't. Maybe I'll get bored of my own complaints, or maybe this is my way of living. As long as it doesn't bother you, why bother? Who knows how long I have got to live? But I'm OK with the way my cognition works with all its imperfections, flaws, sadness, criticism, unwillingness to accept, enthusiasm, pessimism.

November 12, 2010

Imagine you are walking down the road and you don't really know what's waiting for you at the end of the road. At some point, you encounter several obstacles. You think of giving up—you just don't want to continue the journey any longer. So you choose to stop. As far as you can see, there is nothing, absolutely nothing, other than this whatever obstacle (in this case, let's say it's a rock that's thirty metres in height) lying in front of you. God knows how you retain your energy, but let's not go there; that is not the point. Let's be cliché based on the famous "motivational" phrase that "you always have a choice." You can commit suicide by a knife that somehow appears in your pocket, or you can try to climb up the rock. (Again, let's say that some tools suddenly appear to help you.) Climbing the rock is not easy. It's exhausting. It's draining your energy both mentally and physically. What would you choose?

I asked myself about this before and chose to just stop and give up. I have a really low tolerance of stress.

But the thing is that you never know what you are going to find after you overcome that obstacle. I am not a very optimistic person, and I fully acknowledge that after that obstacle, there will just be another one. And another one . . . and another one.

A person with a strong faith, on the other hand, would probably keep going despite having encountered so many obstacles. Why? Perhaps because that person believes that something good will be waiting somewhere down the road. If not, at least that person has tried until the last breath.

If there is one thing I've learned from being here, despite the several mental breakdowns (exaggerating, as usual), is that I have no choice other than to keep moving. Why? Because stopping equals death. I don't want to die just yet.

November 13, 2010

You a prophet, mate? Stop preaching about how people should live their lives. We are all prophets—in our own tiny little paradise that constructs the whole universe. Who are you to condemn?

November 14, 2010

You might find me roaming the streets in shorts and an old T-shirt in daytime, eating food from the vendors. At night, however, it is not impossible to spot me all dressed up, perhaps looking like an entirely different person, somewhere that serves the best martinis and music. No, I am not boasting about the upscale lifestyle or vice versa as I may not know enough. The point I am trying to make is to never judge a person based on one circumstance. What you see is what that person chooses to show at that particular time, but until you've been with that person long enough, you are not in a position to make out a good judgement about them.

I won't deny that I love hedonism—spending money on quality food, drinks, clothes . . . or just for the sake of getting a good atmosphere. I do not see anything wrong with that. It's also not something to necessarily be proud about, though not something to feel guilty about as well. It is just a thing, like playing golf or getting a massage. The stereotype that I often hear is that hedonistic people are merely doing something about their lives. So some people choose to save lives, charities, etc., but doesn't it all come down to personal preferences? I'm sorry if I don't look like I'm doing anything significant to save the planet, but what difference does it make whether I'm going out or staying home? Two different things, same final ends.

And why should someone care about what one does anyway? I know a few who can maintain their academic achievements, while joining some groups to help save the earth and the people in it, and still manage to have a social life. I won't praise or despise them; it is just their personal preferences and perhaps doing so fulfils their needs. Despite having the same basic survival needs, we live in a socially constructed world called society, where nothing is simple. Hence, we all have different needs (which, perhaps, have evolved to "wants"), and just because mine is not in line with yours, it doesn't mean it's a faux pas.

November 25, 2010

My life is in a weird state, but perhaps weird is my normal. I always feel like things don't fit while at the same time they always do. Just because a puzzle is missing one of its pieces, it doesn't mean you can't see the whole picture, right? Though it's better when you have them all. Or is it? Doesn't that empty spot leave a place for imagination? Of course, you can't really picture something that's too far away from the big image, but the details . . . The details are all yours.

The details of my life are all mine to design, though the big outlines are out of my hands. Like painting, maybe, the tools to draw, the skill, and so on are acquired along the way. It's an ongoing process of painting. And learning. Maybe some are so determined to draw a particular picture, inspired by other paintings they stumble upon along the way, working through all the details carefully and precisely. Some, perhaps, are painting as they go, like rubbing your palm against the wall as you walk. (I love doing that!)Nothing's planned; the colours are all picked on the spot, at that very moment.

Or it doesn't have to be that extreme, though I wouldn't call it as being in the grey area. It's more like you don't know what you want but you know what you don't want. I don't know what I would like to paint in my canvas just yet, but I know I like drawing faces. Who knows if I change my mind along the way: black and white or coloured? I only have one canvas, and the size is only limited by my mind.

I thought I have resolved my cognitive dissonance. I thought I have successfully changed the way I thought about *this*. How free are we? All I want to do is curl up and cry, and I have all the free time in the world. I don't want to be invisible. I want to disappear, even from my own mind. Invisible means you're still there, among everybody, but no one can see you. I don't want to not just be seen. I don't want to feel, know, or be.

December 4, 2010

I am now becoming increasingly scared of *really* telling how I feel here. It's like running naked in public. You let yourself become so exposed when you really have no reason to.

December 8, 2010

I always have mixed feelings about everything, including being home. I felt like I haven't come home in years, though it's only been three months. When I stepped out of the plane, I was grinning like a stupid kid, and then I realised I wouldn't be coming back to the images of home I had had in mind. Things are different now—people have changed—and then it saddened me. This is the fourth day I'm here, and I haven't even seen anyone. I only came out of the house to do some errands. My life isn't exactly the same as it was two years ago.

Well, I mean, you should embrace change, right? Easier said than done. It's like my life is in a constant motion of extreme changes. It was hard enough to adapt with Canberra, and the only thing available to hold on to was this concept of home far, far away, and that was supposed to stay constant. Now that it's not even the same, I'm slowly losing my grip. And I know that I should stop taking into account the stupid little things and start looking at the overall picture, but I can't just pick what to think about and what not. I guess the only thing that is constant is change indeed.

So what is being home?

I wish I were more rootless, you know, so it's easier not to get attached then get all lost when the roots are finally dead and I have to look for somewhere to plant new seeds on.

December 9, 2010

I am torn between acting and holding back. If only we live for ourselves alone. What is freedom when I have mine and you have yours, and we live in this clustered world? Isn't "social freedom" some sort of oxymoron? How do you define "free" in a social world? Everything has its own price, and I can't decide if this theory of social exchange really works. So here I am, sitting and waiting, until my time comes.

December 10, 2010

Another new prescription. Wanna bet? I doubt it'll work.

Early morning is like greeting an old friend I know all too well. Those moments before you drift into sleep, you become your own worst enemy. All those thoughts you try so hard to suppress—you have nowhere to hide. How do you escape from your own mind? If only I could build an unsolvable maze in my head that I myself could not even solve.

Confronting. Yeah, easy to say. What if you don't even know what to confront? It's intangible, yet you know it's there. It's the little voice that tells you, "This isn't right. Or wrong. Can't tell the difference."

You make peace with yourself, and then you realise peace only exists in conjunction with suffering. One cannot exist without the other, regardless of which comes first. I'm sick of people preaching about making peace with yourself, that happiness is within you, that you need to forgive yourself and then others, that what is absolute is the divine.

"Suffering and happiness are all in your head." True, all true. The problem is sometimes you just really don't know what is it that you're looking for, or hiding from, but you just keep going. And how? Accepting things the way they are? I wouldn't be here if I was so happy with the way things were. But then, am I progressing? Where to? Does it matter? Happiness and suffering are not just simple, absolute entities. They stem from so many things. One leads to another like a fucking giant spider web.

And in a different state of mind, I once wrote that being sad about change is like regretting the fact that trees grow. If you say you can just force yourself to accept it, to apply any techniques of justifying or some sort, if you think that thinking about death is stupid, then you clearly have never been in anyone else's shoes but yours. Just because you've never experienced it, it doesn't mean it doesn't exist. Oh, what the hell. Who am I to know, and who are you to judge?

December 11, 2010

I was secretly scared that while I'm gone, things would change drastically. Oh, dear self-fulfilling prophecy. Things always turn out the way you expect them to be. Well, most of the times. I'm secretly anxious every time I see people. It's like meeting new people all over again while in fact I've known them for years. You know how when you really do know each other, no matter how long you haven't seen each other, you would just pick up a conversation where it left off?

I guess we all change. I have changed, they've changed, and things have changed. I tried so hard to hold back my tears when I saw those three towers. Not because I was embarrassed to cry but because I thought I really should start embracing change. I mean, every single thing has changed. I used to be able to come home at whatever hour. Now at eleven something, someone gets all suspicious and thinks I might be doing drugs. It's so hard to bear the loss of something (the freedom) that has shaped you. It's like you can feel a part of your body is missing, but you can't really know what it is. I am the way I am because of what I've been through, and changing it all in one night is impossible. Not to mention it hurts.

Would it be easier if I hadn't had it all? So I wouldn't miss what I had?

December 29, 2010

Drowning provides some kind of comfort to me. It's a place where nobody else wants to go to or be in a state of. Its silence is a break. You can find out just how long you're able to survive before you run out of breath. And for once, there is no distraction at all.

December 30, 2010

Can't expect much, you know. When you expect, you hurt. As it goes, as we go.

January 1, 2011

I want to disappear.

Every day, I recite the same prayer—not necessarily a good one. Every day, during the day, I thank the one whom I pray to that it's not granted. At night, I recite the same prayer, again. I have got to stop this.

January 3, 2011

I'm hurting people. I'm making a fool out of myself. I set a limit then I crossed it. I hate self-pity, but I can't help thinking that sometimes I'm this irreparable mess that does nothing but hurt anything around me.

One minute I'm on top of the world, and the next I'm an outcast, even in my own world. A stranger, someone I can barely recognize. A familiar face I know nothing about inside.

I lost count of those I've tried. Nothing worked. Nothing.

January 4, 2011

And this too shall pass. I've got to get myself together.

January 5, 2011

I think it's true that we need to have aspirations, both long term and short term. You need to wake up looking forward to something, if not something small. It's bad enough to wake up to nothing, let alone to avoid something that is part of your responsibility. I have decided to live day to day, to achieve something small. A goal I set for myself daily

I still owe a certain someone that one long-distance phone call. I'm just not sure if I'm ready for it. It will either be a total silence or a full-on mumbling and sobbing.

We're born alone; we die alone. In-between, you feel alone. You don't have to, but you do. Unfortunately, we can't choose what to feel. No, I won't argue with anyone on that. I cannot choose what to feel, and this is by far my hardest battle with myself. I feel things that I shouldn't feel, or perhaps not feel what I *should* feel.

Of course, I won't leave out the good ones in-between. Loneliness isn't so alone. After all, what is loneliness without ever experiencing the opposite? But the truth is, good or bad, they never complement each other—they substitute. I can't remember the last time I felt happy. When I was happy, I couldn't remember the last time I felt sad.

January 6, 2011

Because death has no analogies, and meanings are limited to our own imaginations—or our own manifestations of our own ideals, expectations, and insecurities (about death).

Can we ever really grasp the feel of death, unless we're dead? But once you're dead, you unify with death; you become death. Death is you; you are dead.

Does language limit our ability to express or feel, or is it a tool to help fulfil our limited attempt to grasp something that is not tangible and explainable? Does attaching meaning to things help us to know (and what is *to know?*), or does it just satisfy our need to know—only with the illusion of knowing?

January 7, 2011

All those thoughts, encrypted by silence. Sometimes, words are not capable enough to convey. Words simplify—too simplified of the real. Can you read my silence? Fortunately, we aren't all mind readers. Where else can we hide if not in our own silence?

Is silence merely the absence of words, or does it stand on its own feet? Can I explain right without the presence of left?

January 12, 2011

Do you (really) believe that things happen for a reason? That there is no such thing as "random coincidences"?

I have been trying to keep my emotions at arm's length, but how am I supposed to do that when everything that has happened prevents me to do so?

I do believe that people come into your life as teachers. I may not be a good student, but one thing I've learned is that when they have decided to leave, letting go becomes the only option.

Unfortunately, sometimes the lesson is only learned long after the teacher has gone.

January 25, 2011

The constant headaches, trembling hands, and thoughts running at a speed of light; euphoria and exhaustion. What exactly am I exhausted from? It's like running from an invisible figure.

Am I running from it or towards it?

It's as if there's this hole that I've tried to fill in with so many things, but nothing fits. But do we ever really know what is it we're searching for? Are we sort of in a journey where we don't know where and how it ends?

"Just be." Yeah, easy to say. Be what? One second, I'm this nonstop talker, and the next, I feel like burying myself deep in the earth's deepest crust. Then I give myself a mental slap, telling myself that I should not be complaining. A complainer by nature—will I ever be satisfied?

Aren't we all continually changing—what is changing? Aren't we the makers and the destroyers? Aren't we both the creations and the creators?

The lovers and the haters of the same things?

Aren't people funny? We're hurt by the ones we love the most, because we love them. What is hate without love? One minute you feel secure, but the feeling of losing that sense of security ironically chains you, turns you into this creature you don't even recognise. But it's you, and it's me. Do mirrors lie?

Why these contradictions?

January 28, 2011

How could you wake up in the morning indifferent to the beauty of the sun, the fresh morning air, and the comfort of your sofa, while on the next day—same shit every day—you could wake up feeling like you've been hit by a miracle, and you're grateful for being alive?

How could you wholeheartedly laugh during the day and shed endless tears to sleep during the bleakness of the night?

I didn't sign up for a roller-coaster ride.

February 11, 2011

I've always thought of myself as being in the grey area, but perhaps that wasn't always the case. After all, five days of being hospitalised made me realise that maybe I've always been in one or the other—black and white—and it's tiring the fuck out of me. So now I have two choices:

1. Stabilizers. As I said, they'd make me feel flat and empty. No despair, no happiness. A walking zombie.
2. Keeping things the way they are with a healthier diet and lifestyle.

This is confusing . . . How?

I feel like digging my own grave.

February 18, 2011

So you think you know, but how much do you really know? Can you really rely on your own interpretations?

So you think you're better than some people in some ways, but how much do you really know about those you're comparing yourself to? We all are fighting our own battle.

My battle isn't exactly your battle, so no one ever wins, and no one ever loses.

February 28, 2011

"These mood swings can include irritability, energetic happiness, impulsive and erratic behaviour, deep depression, anger, or even agitated confusion . . ."

I guess doctors wouldn't prescribe certain meds with no certain reasons, after all.

I don't know why self-diagnosing can be so addictive . . . innate need of explanations?

But things are more stable now, inside, though the recent physical outburst sort of crept out. I hope it won't happen again, although I still don't remember a thing. I still laugh every time my mom told me the story, as if it happened to someone else, despite my mom's traumatic face when telling it.

March 1, 2011

Last night I had a dream where a novelist shot me on the back of my head with a gun while I was reading his book. Then I became I wandering ghost and met other ghosts who died from reading his book like me.

Did not see the novelist's face. I remember the fear though.

I wish I had a more entertaining imagination.

March 2, 2011

I hate reading my own writing, especially the published ones. I hate hearing my own voice in the recording, especially for interviews. I hate looking at tagged photos. I hate seeing me from someone else's eyes.

March 17, 2011

I'm secretly scared that you might have been right. Perhaps that's why I hate reading my writings so much, because deep down I know it wasn't me. It wasn't me in the recordings; it wasn't me writing all that crap and interviews. Perhaps that's why I was so defensive about it. I know, and it scares the hell out of me. It breaks the whole security web I have been stitching for quite some time now. I have been resting under the shadow of my own doubt.

But was it not me, or was it the true me? Or both? I wish switching was far easier than having to bear with all the consequences, not being able to recall memories, getting hospitalized, losing some of the most important things in my life. To be frank, was it all worth it? Would I come this far without it? Would I be better off without it?

Two months ago, today's me would look at "me" and say, "You're a mess." Am I now?

March 21, 2011

To be honest, the safest place at the moment is this city. Its lack of people is an advantage. Its silence is bliss. Its inaccessibility is a blessing.

March 22, 2011

Is it possible that this feeling of gratefulness arises like a boomerang that keeps coming back, ever so demanding? To long for that feeling, like hands softly touching and seducing, knocking from inside of the memory? To be back, but to where? I know that some place exists inside the memory, but it's not the same anymore. It has passed. Five seconds ago, five hours, a year, what difference does it make? The fact is still true: it has passed.

At moments like this, I am angry with the present. It's as if it is instilled in my mind to play the game of blame, but on what? Change? It's like being angry with a silent tree, a tree that is ten times larger than my body. The tree will answer with its silence all my questions, and it will stand still, unmoved by my anger.

The great ones are the ones that hurt the most. The great ones blind us to the present—comparison kills. How can we hold on so tightly to a time in the past? What makes it so hard to let go? Some say that everything is beautiful, if only we could swap our glasses—our lenses through which we see the world. If only feeling, or not feeling, is as easy as closing and opening our eyes.

How do you define acceptance? I'm scared that if I loosen my grip, the memory will soon become insignificant, fade away. I don't want to get hurt and haunted by the beauty of the past, but at the same time, I don't want its value to become less. I don't want to forget. But how can I feel the beauty of other things if I'm still holding on so tightly to the past? I've only got two hands.

March 25, 2011

It's unfortunate to realise that it's the roller-coaster ride that evokes so much. I am on stable ground; I don't know whether I should consider it good or bad. What can I say about stability? First, it makes my sleeping pattern less chaotic. Second, those who are the closest wouldn't have to deal with my tantrums. Third, it means I screw up less. Fourth, I'm less irritated—less, not absolute.

March 27, 2011

I never thought I'd jump from 10,000 feet. I'm still scared of heights, of course, but when you see that there's nothing under your feet and you're in the clouds, it's nothing like I've ever imagined it would be.

March 28, 2011

Physical pain is there to alarm us where the body is injured and needs to be protected in order to recover. In calmness, we retreat to recover from the pain, the hurt. But we can't stay still forever, for eventually the pain subsides, the storm passes, and the night comes to an end. It is in-between the two extremes that harmony can be found. Suffering only exists in conjunction with peace and happiness, just as life is defined by death.

What is a start without an end? What is love without pain? Change is the only thing that is constant, indeed. After the storm, the sun will rise again. We sleep and we wake up; the eyes close and open again. And someday, our eyes will close forever; our gaze will drift into eternal sleep. The end of the rhythm is what makes it a complete symphony

March 29, 2011

I wonder what it would be like if you were still alive. It's weird how after someone died, the memory of them stayed the same while everything around you changed. People around me change—hell, I've changed. I can picture the transition of every one of them over time. But you are just how I remember, every time. Maybe because I didn't get to know that much, so I'm just picking up pieces of memories I can recall.

I wonder what you'd say if you were to see me today. Would you still say the same thing you did? Or would you be proud? I wish we had more conversations. Maybe you could have told your stories, like what you were like when you were young, what sort of music you listened to, why you decided to convert, or how you see life. Maybe I could tell you what it was like growing up as a teenager, and now I can tell you how I see me at that time, and maybe we could finally agree on some things.

But the moments have passed and you can't turn back time. It's like looking at an unfinished painting, but maybe God decided that what seems to be unfinished is actually finished . . . just as it is.

April 1, 2011

So we all have our own "unique" zigzags. Clashes or you fit mine. No zags can fit perfectly, and I don't know any life key-cutting service here. You can't add; you can only cut. You're gonna lose some part of you. We're all cutting ourselves away.

April 2, 2011

I wish for so many things that I used to have.

April 3, 2011

The existence of God is an issue that has been debated over a long period of time. However, just like most philosophical issues, nothing can really be conclusive, probably because nothing can undisputedly be used as evidence to prove or disprove God's existence. Many theists believe in God based on faith, although faith itself never provides any answer, just a willingness to believe without sufficient evidence. The case of God's existence becomes interesting because it is a belief that is often taken for granted. It is also interesting how people can have different ideas of God and how God can become a major, or minor, part in people's lives. The majority of theists believe in God simply because their beliefs on the existence of God have been instilled in their minds since they were young and therefore it becomes difficult to believe otherwise. Both atheists and theists have many arguments to support their position, but the strongest would be the design argument and the problem of evil.

The design argument is by far the strongest argument for the existence of God. The design argument, also known as the teleological argument, states that this world is designed by a designer whom we call God. The argument was first introduced by St Thomas Aquinas in The Five Ways as the fifth way of proving the existence of God. Aquinas stated that things generally have similar mechanisms or act in the same manners and they tend to converge towards a common goal. I read somewhere that the whole point of this kind of argument is simply that there can be no design without a designer, and if the designer has decided to create a design, then it must be done for a purpose. The argument is also commonly explained by the analogy of a creation, such as a building needs an architect, a watch requires a watchmaker, a piece of clothing requires a designer, and so on. Hence, based on that analogy, it is assumed that the universe must be designed by something bigger than the universe itself, which is God, and that the universe was created for a purpose or a goal. Stanley, or someone, stated the design argument that states that obtaining further knowledge is always dependent upon past knowledge. Therefore, obtaining intelligence must require earlier intelligence. If man is able to obtain knowledge, something must have created the previous knowledge, and if the chain goes on backwards, there must be something that has originated the subsequent knowledge.

However, many people are still not convinced of God's existence. The problem of evil has raised many questions and doubt against the existence of God. The problem is stated as a contradiction between the existence of both evil and a benevolent and powerful God. Some theists argue that evil arises from the consequences of human's free will, but it seems very hard to understand how a benevolent and powerful God can create such evil, which results in human suffering. McCloskey Something—I can't remember his name—stated in his article on God and evil that there are two general kinds of evil, namely "physical" and "moral" evil. Physical evils, also known as natural evils, occur within the earth and animal kingdom. These kinds of evil are caused by the natural phenomenon, such as natural disaster, diseases, and physical deformities and defects. A powerful God should be able to prevent, or at least stop, natural evils from occurring. A benevolent God should also not allow moral evils, which are simply immoralities, such as selfishness, envy, greed, deceit, cruelty, callousness, and cowardice, and when they are combined, may lead to wars. Horrible events, such as diseases, natural disasters, and wars, can still be found today. The problem of evil is therefore real and thus means that evil and God are incompatible, since evil contradicts with power and benevolence of God. But what is evil? How can you define something that's evil other than causing human suffering? Can evil be justified in any ways?

The problem of evil has often troubled thoughtful believers, causing many to convert into atheism or agnosticism, especially those who have witnessed or suffered evil in their lives. Stelee questioned God, in his book on atheism, by stating that God, who is benevolent and powerful, is supposed to be benevolent towards humans, or at least to those who believe in His goodness. If God is supposed to be all powerful and benevolent, then He should be able to diminish all the evil occurring or to never create evil at all, and humans' free will cannot explain or resolve this contradiction. Free will may be able to explain the occurrence of moral evil, but physical evil does not seem to relate with free will. Theists have also come up with another defence by stating that suffering or pain creates the greater good. This "greater good" defence claims that a person's suffering provides an opportunity for another person to act towards goodness to help. However, the extent of the pain and suffering seems "excessive, prolonged, and unnecessary." Why does God need to six million people to be killed by the Nazis, for example, in order to create the greater good? Besides, people are still fighting in wars in this modern time, which shows that the goodness created is not enough to prevent evil from reoccurring. According to some guy I read somewhere, some theists have tried to overcome the problem of evil by declaring it as a mystery that humans are not able to explain. This argument does not seem to provide any logical and intelligent answer at all; it even raises more confusion. The problem of evil therefore is still a big issue facing humans today, which contradicts the most important aspects of God: his power and benevolence.

The most famous evidence against the design argument is the evolution theory proposed by Darwin 150 years ago in *On the Origin of Species.* The evolution theory states that evolution is an ongoing process that includes natural selections and adaptations, which explains why things have become the way they are today. Although it seems that the evolution does not support the design argument, science actually provides evidence to show that evolution *does* support the design argument. Every creature in the universe seems to point to a well-designed hierarchy that would not make sense without a grand designer. If there is no such grand designer, instead of systematic evolution, chaos and disorder would have taken place, as things would move in a highly random manner.

Evolutionary biology actually supports the design argument. He explained that teleological explanations are appropriate in certain areas of natural science. A teleological explanation is where an object's existence is explained by the connection between the object's state to its surroundings and that the object is acting towards a certain goal or end state. This kind of explanation can be found in the human body, namely the homeostatic reactions. The homeostatic reactions are responsible in maintaining the body system, such as the body temperature, so that an organism may survive and adapt within its surroundings. Moreover, the human body is physically designed to perform a certain function, just as the human eye is designed to see. Natural selections can account for the presence of homeostatic mechanisms. This shows how one thing leads to another, contributing to a bigger purpose. Someone therefore concluded that teleological mechanisms in living mechanisms are thus biological adaptations. Moser and Kopan also stated in their book on theism that scientists have increasingly come to realise how the initial conditions of the universe and the basic constants of physics must be balanced for intelligent lives to evolve, which is exactly the same as the "fine-tuning" of the cosmos. Evolutionary biology is hence proven to support the design theory by showing that each mechanism or adaptation is contributing to a bigger goal or purpose.

Although science has come up with reasons for the existence of God, it is still not absolute evidence to prove the absolute existence of God. I read someone stated in his article on existence that "existence" itself cannot be deduced or derived from thought by any purely logical processes. It seems to me that God is just merely an idea, argued and supported by suppositions and assumptions. Also, even if there is a God, the problem of evil has been a major cause of my doubts against the benevolent God and still has not been resolved until now. Witnessing so much human suffering in the world makes it hard not to question God's existence. A lot of people still seek His help to ease their burden, but many of their prayers are left unanswered. But with the problem of evil, it makes me think, *How do we define benevolent without the presence of weakness? How is humanity defined?*

April 4, 2011

I'm angry. I'm so irritable to the point that I hate myself for being so pissed off all the time. I'm trying not to let it show, but it's crawling under my skin and sometimes it leaks. I got pissed off at the guy at the traffic light who insisted to clean my window despite the fact that I said no. I got so pissed to the point I almost cried while driving, then I felt guilty for not giving him a dollar because he looked so miserable. I got angry when my mom insisted that it was the right antenna cable while it wasn't. I sort of yelled at the big w guy, and I regret doing so. I am so mad at you from doing what you did and at me for doing what I did and the fact that I sort of miss you. And it hurts, because I, again, lost something so important and I am left with the stupid memories that I wish I can erase. But then every time I wish to erase them, I get into a fight with myself, which always ends up with me getting all lost in them. I am irritated with someone who overimpersonates, although I have no right for being mad at it. I am so pissed off at a certain someone who gave me some responsibilities that I wasn't told about, such a one-sided decision. Please don't do that again. I am trying not to let my anger out on you. I am angry with my incapability of saying no despite my overloading assignments to do. I am angry with the fact that I am stuck and I don't know how to get out of this without hurting anybody.

April 5, 2011

If it's true that when you die your whole life flashes before your eyes, I have thought of some moments that might definitely come up. Have you ever thought about your own death or how it'll take place? Not in a suicidal way though, just out of curiosity. I reckon that those four years will definitely flash in details, depending on how much time I'll have.

I've lost four. I know I shouldn't have done some of the things I did. Missing something only hurts when you can't gain it back, and this is my hell. If your hell is to get yourself burned in hell, this is hell on earth. Maybe I'm exaggerating, but you don't know how the cycle goes. Doctors love you because you are living proof of their normality. You're a wreck, and they're there to fix. It's a different world inside and outside the room. You sit and you tell your life stories and they take notes, the support of their judgement. Once you're this, then the next you're another.

They're more normal than you. Once you step into that room, there must be something wrong with you. The wrongness of you that they read somewhere in their textbooks during college. They checklist the symptoms that they aren't personally familiar with. But you yearn for explanations, for answers, why you're the way you are. They give you information by the meds you're given. You self-diagnose. Misleading.

Or you can always resort to being your own doctor. You indulge in whatever meds you give yourself. Consume until you're consumed.

Then you're back again in the room, until an hour is up.

April 7, 2011

Nothing pisses me off more than ignorant people who underestimate what someone else is going through. Have you ever tried to swim in their pool of emotions or put yourself in their shoes? To give the most shallow, ignorant piece of mind of what it's like inside of someone else's jar while you're standing outside of it is just . . . ignorant. And to think that you know what it feels like to walk in their shoes while you've never even walked barefoot is just . . .

At least think before you speak, you know, or at least try. Digest what the other is saying instead of just replying with whatever comes into your mind. If you are not in a position to give a piece of your judgement, then keep it to yourself. Don't make someone else's day worse than it already is.

April 10, 2011

I don't feel angry, but little things seem to get on my nerves so easily these days. I may need to cancel a thing or two, postpone a thing or two, end a thing or two, and deal with a prolonged unresolved thing or two.

Or two or more. I have decided to stop making myself miserable as I have been for the last couple of weeks, the time which I have spent revisiting inviting memories. I realise that memories can be warmer than reality due to many, too many, reasons.

So I was thinking, *Why have I been playing all these different roles lately?* I mean, of course we all do: a daughter, a son, a student, a sibling, a customer, an assistant, a whiner . . . on the same day. But I have been playing different types of ex—ex-this, ex-that—and I was stuck in different times where I was on top of my world.

But what if it's a flat line? I was never on the top of the mountain or on the bottom of the river. There is no mountain or river, only land.

I have been making myself so miserable, and I have been blaming the world for making myself miserable, only to realise that everything stayed the same. Well, not you, clearly, but the things I thought were making me miserable. I have repeated the word *miserable* so many times now it feels like it doesn't mean anything anymore.

You meant the world, but every time I miss you, I guess I just miss the time when you meant the world to me.

April 14, 2011

We manipulate our reality. We all do. Let me tell you about a little girl who needed to make sense of her world, because no one would tell her what was going on. Now that she's finally standing on her own feet, could anyone blame her for how she sees the world the way it is?

That girl is in all of us, and we're pissed creatures. One day she finds someone who sees the same way she does, and then they're both pissed. The world naked isn't fun to look at, or maybe we're just used to putting on clothes. Everything is fashion . . . our helpless attempt to beautify reality.

I can't hold on forever to it, you know. We've come this far, but for all I know, this can be the end of the journey. Let's just think of it that way. It saves me so much trouble. So I'm getting up with my bag on and I will put the book in my bag. Just knowing that I'll be able to read a chapter or two is enough for now. I can pick the ones I want to read—maybe I'll be able to feel the way I want to feel. Who knows?

April 17, 2011

You lie. You lie all the time. You lie about little things. You lie to yourself to make yourself feel better when things clearly aren't. Then it gets worse. Then you lie again: "Well, I . . . but . . ."

What's going to happen when you stop lying? Because the truth is there no truth, then a lie is the truth. Bend everything.

When you're hurt, you lie. "Well, maybe it wasn't meant to be." When will you stop blaming fate? Fate is the lamest justification that ever existed.

April 18, 2011

I'm tired. I can't sleep. Don't look at me as if I'm on anything. I'm tired with all these cycles. It's either I'm six feet under or I'm a minister of my own kingdom. It aches everywhere. I just need to sleep, please. You doctors give meds, but in my eyes, your years spent in med school are such a waste. I lost count of the things that I had been told by you to digest. Well, I am still the same as I was when I was a kid, or a teen, or whatever it is twenty counts as.

You think I'm a mess. You think I plan to be this way? It's not a recreational ride, it's not fun. It's not like Disneyland or something where you get to pick the ride. One minute your dead bored stuck in a merry go round and the next you're fucking upside down in a roller coaster that's not moving.

April 22, 2011

And then one day you just find yourself in the middle of nowhere you know. You don't even remember how you got here, and here you are. You aren't happy or dissatisfied. You just are, or aren't, if you prefer.

How the hell did I end up here? Then suddenly, I start comparing. I wish comparing would make me feel grateful, but no. Or maybe I have just picked up the wrong ones. Stagnant. I was wandering around alone, and then all of a sudden, I decided to cut my hair. Never planned to. All of a sudden, I felt like I needed a change in my life. I thought cutting my hair would have been pretty a radical one . . . Ha ha ha. Now it's too short, but oh, well. As long as my heart is still beating, the rest of the system will too, right? Hair grows, big deal. *bitter smile*

I used to worry. A lot. Now I say a lot of wrong things, or most of the things I say aren't the ones I mean for people to hear. But hey, life is a series of experiments, right?

April 24, 2011

Did you know that first-class lounges are always the loneliest places out of the whole terminal? It's not that I'm bragging about anything; I'm flying economy, of course. Me getting to be here is one of the advantages and disadvantages of having a world-travelling mom.

When I was a kid and still underage, my mom always brought me to these sorts of place as her plus one. She always travels business, rarely first unless upgraded, and it's paid by the company anyway. And I always travel economy. The peak hour here is between eight and twelve—I don't know why. Don't know much about flight schedules. Of the boarding passes these people hold, 80 percent are business class, 10 to 15 percent are economy class, and very rarely, I see first-class passengers lounging here. I think they might even have gotten bored with all the phony, expensive, ordinary, and cold furniture anyways. Maybe.

Most of the people here are middle-aged men with business suits. There are only two people at the restaurant: me and this white, middle-aged man who looks tired and spaced out. He's eating sushi, but his eyes aren't looking at the sushi, the plate, or the hand. I don't know what he's thinking about—maybe nothing. Maybe he's fed up with thinking. So he's eating his sushi now while waiting for his next flight.

Sometimes, I see a woman or two among these men. I have always been the youngest here, I think. Maybe I don't deserve to be here anyway. Well, most of the people who hold first-class tickets are usually the ones who are least likely for you to expect to be first-class passengers . . . or maybe it's just me. They're the most laidback ones. They don't even care if their clothes don't match. Sometimes, they even look like lost tourists. Mostly, however, around 90 percent of these people are incredibly old, and the rest are super clean-cut, Armani suit businessmen . . . or just rich men. I don't know.

But this is so quiet, too quiet sometimes. There's always the free-flow bar, of course, where you can act like a stressed-out person who sits at the bar alone while the bartender keeps pouring drinks into your empty glass.

When I was a kid, I used to be so excited about all the free food, free ice cream, the coffee machines, the free drinks (not that kind of drinks and I wasn't allowed to drink coffee, of course). Now I'm just indifferent. I'd rather be spending my time browsing around.

I don't know what I am doing here. What am I doing here?

April 25, 2011

So many meds every freaking day, I'm starting to get a little bit fed up. Not to mention the more extreme cycles. Last night I had another crying spell at the lounge. I couldn't stop even after the plane took off. It would have been comforting if I had only known the reason *why*. I didn't. Drained the hell out of me. So I took some and it made me fall asleep, and as usual, *"Everything will be better in the morning. It always is."*

April 27, 2011

So I stopped trying. I stopped trying to make things right. I stopped trying to fix some things. Maybe they're meant to be left broken—maybe broken is perfection. I now wear the first clothes I touch and see. No more changing and changing and changing. I stopped sugar-coating—words, feelings, everything. If my truth conflicts with yours, then oh, well. I stopped trying to feel what I want to feel; I welcome the sadness and the pain, only to realise they're the only way to really appreciate happiness when it comes. When I try so hard to feel happy when I actually don't, it becomes superficial. I hate being superficial, but that's just what I want myself to be. When I want myself to be a particular thing, I become what I hate the most: *superficial.*

April 30, 2011

Since I was little until now, there have been days when I have woken up feeling excited for no apparent reason. I would then find a reason for my excitement, starting from a new stationary, perhaps, and if I had none, I would just hope that something exciting would happen during the day. Most of the time, however, nothing exciting would happen. I forgot the excitement during the day anyway. It eroded.

Those days stopped for a year or two, and now I'm having one of those days again. It's good. It's good waking up feeling good and not going to bed feeling like shit. Sometimes, it's like waking up from a really good dream and the excitement follows, only to realise it's real life. I wake up and I go on hoping something exciting will happen. One day I woke up feeling excited and my car broke down, but I didn't go to bed feeling like shit. So it's still good, right?

Maybe it's a gift from my curse. My curse has its perks, you know? I like the perks, though this won't be what I'll be saying when I'm in a different state. Or I can think of it as a gift and this is the curse. My "gift" and its curse, its curse for leaving me feel all excited when there's nothing to be excited about except for my mere existence. Then I go and think about the good days, and it makes me feel a bit sad. I go on and hope something exciting will happen, because I want to escape from feeling nostalgic.

May 2, 2011

I miss my safety net . . . or I miss the time when I had a safety net. It's as if you just ignore the hair falling out until you have no more hair to lose. I have a feeling that this is not going to be a good year. Didn't start off well, but I still hope and pray it's going to be a good one. It's just sometimes some feelings just won't go away, no matter how hard you want them to, or maybe it's the trying that ruins everything.

Where have I been? I feel like I've just woken up to a really good dream, and now it's gone.

May 3, 2011

Hello. It's downhill again. Like what doc told me: identify and welcome. If I had known, I would have been able to tell you this; please bear with me. But you couldn't bear it, could you? Well, I almost couldn't.

I am waiting for something exciting to happen. I am waiting for something exciting to happen. I am waiting for something exciting to happen. I am waiting for something exciting to happen. I am waiting for something exciting to happen. I am waiting for something exciting to happen.

May 4, 2011

I am waiting for something exciting to happen. I am waiting for something exciting to happen. I am waiting for something exciting to happen. I am waiting for something exciting to happen. I am waiting for something exciting to happen. I am waiting for something exciting to happen. I am waiting for something exciting to happen. I am waiting for something exciting to happen. I am waiting for something exciting to happen. I am waiting for something exciting to happen.

Just one of those feelings. Again. I've checked my phones so many times already. Nothing. I even checked Facebook, inboxes, the mailbox, tumblr. Nothing. Yet I am still waiting for something exciting to happen. This is just sad. Mania. Mania. Mania. Is it?

May 8, 2011

Which one hurts the most? Geographical distance or emotional distance?

Which one hurts less? When you're not geographically far but you know that the other person is no longer emotionally there, or when you are apart but you know that the other person is emotionally longing for you? Or when you're apart, you don't know whether the other person is still there or not. You jump in with eyes closed, hoping you won't hit anything hard.

I am so homesick, but home in a time that's passed.

May 9, 2011

I miss the time when crying was so easy when I wanted to. Now it's as if something is compressing my lachrymal glands. I've tried watching sad movies, sad TV series, even sad clips on YouTube, but I just can't. My eyes get glassy at best. It's not that I'm being dramatic or want to be dramatic, but something is dying to be cried out loud. Until I can cry, I'm like a sick person with mucus on the chest, coughing while hoping to get the mucus out. I know that's a disgusting metaphor, but it represents it best.

Why are we the way we are? I hope for a more stable personality, but this is the best I can get. I signed up for get up and go, OK. It's progress. Do you get bored when things are too stable? Or are you content? I don't know what to feel, really. It's as if I'm both happy and a mess. A happy mess. No, a happy and sad mess. My current state of mind is like a messy wardrobe.

I wish I was more organized too. Why can't I be organized? It's weird how when I meet organized men, it reminds me of a reversed gender role.

May 10, 2011

Years ago seem like yesterday, and so much has changed. Things are still changing; I'm still changing. We've lost and gained. Some things we hoped to stay. They didn't. It hurts when I think about how much I've taken for granted. I've never realised they were gone until they are now. But I learn from the things I've lost. I learn from my loss. I didn't learn from them when they were still there. Maybe learning is part of my self-defence mechanism. After all, I don't want an absolute loss. The least I can gain is a lesson to not take things for granted in the future. But am I really learning? I might be taking some things for granted as I'm typing now, as I'm remembering what I've lost.

Maybe I should start seeing loss as something else. I'm standing on a platform and watching all these trains come and go without stepping in one. Each train has all these images of the past, of the things I was once in. I was in it, but the doors have closed forever. So I turn my back and get on to the train that has no images.

It's moments like these when we stand on a platform, when we detach from the present and look at the bigger picture of our lives.

May 11, 2011

I didn't plan to live my life this way. I never planned to have waves coming and going. Waves of melancholy, waves of euphoria. Some know why they feel a certain way; some others don't. My battle is struggling to move back and forth; my feelings swing like a pendulum. Some days I wake up with excitement even though the days end the same way like any other days. Some other days, I wake up regretting my existence. Some days I fall asleep smiling; other days I fall asleep crying. The thing is I never know why. Not everything has an answer. Their answers can seem unacceptable sometimes. It's their truth, not mine.

Or I know why. They say it's genetics. They say it's psychological. They say it's embedded in my genes. And they try to fix it chemically. Sometimes, the waves make me feel blessed; sometimes, they bring my energy with them. They leave me drained, dried out, empty. Sometimes, they bring with them the hurt and the pain, leaving me at ease. Sometimes, I don't want these waves to come when things are at their best, but this is how things go in my castle that I built with sand. Each wave that comes crushes the walls of my castle. I am standing there naked, trying to rebuild my castle, my kingdom, my home. Some days I rebuild it happily; some days I give up—homeless.

May 14, 2011

What happens when you're stuck with your own interpretation that sets you in pain? How do you deal with pain? How do you *justify* pain? How do you justify anything, really? I told myself to welcome pain and to experience every detail, to immerse myself in it, but that's not easy. Immersing myself in pain is like agreeing to be stabbed with a thousand needles. Is that a choice though? Will I ever be able to see things the way they are if I keep protecting myself?

Some people told me that in some periods of time, I'm a mess. A wreck. But what do they know? Maybe I like switching back and forth between being a mess and a clean sheet. Maybe I'm a mess because when I'm a mess my world turns into something different. Though I do ask myself sometimes whether the difference is worth the consequences. I don't care about one-time judgements, really. I don't wish you to know me better than that anyway. I don't want you to.

May 16, 2011

There's this hole. I don't know how it got there, but there's this hole. I don't even know exactly where it is, but I know it's there. It's like I'm missing out on something. I don't even know what I'm missing out on. Nothing I do feels right.

I hate this feeling. The feeling of being an outcast, of living in someone else's world. I feel lost. I feel dumbfounded. I wish I were clementine because right now memories hurt; the present hurts because it's related to the past. I feel like sleeping forever.

May 18, 2011

I kept telling myself to get a new book. I told myself it was time to start writing a new book. Then I found myself rereading the same old chapter over and over again. I hate myself for doing so. But how do we know when it's the right time? Maybe there is never a right time.

You can only get hurt by what you love. The greater the love, the greater the hurt, the greater the satisfaction and dissatisfaction.

The greater the risk, the greater the price, and the loss. Love is like gambling; your heart is your bet. I don't like gambling, as I don't like losing. Sadly, losing is part of winning. You never know how winning feels without ever losing anything. I'm not keen on winning, I hate competitions. But life is a competition against time, pain, and yourself.

May 19, 2011

I don't wake up feeling excited anymore, but I feel sleepy. I feel sleepy all the time. I'm mentally OK, I think, I just can't resist the urge to sleep. I space out during classes. I yawned in front of my tutors—I can't help it. I know this is how my days will be like for at least another two weeks. I have a name now. This is the sleecle. Yesterdays were the manic, they say. Now I feel sleepy, but the sleep at night is bad. Every two or three months, I get a different life. I will get them back though, in two or three months. I hated it at first, but I've decided to make peace with it. I'll still complain in one of those days, of course, but at times like these, I will make peace, because wars are tiring. I just want peace.

May 20, 2011

I don't adapt well to changes, hence the delayed everything. When I experience something that's too much, whatever it is, the happiness or the pain, will be delayed. Maybe it's part of my psychological immune system, to protect from feeling too much. This is why the inappropriate emotions are shown at the wrong time. I didn't cry at the funeral. I felt nothing. Years later, I cried like a little baby. I only experienced the loss years later. Here I am, months later, just beginning to hate you. I honestly didn't feel anything, but now I do. I'm just beginning to digest everything. Now I understand why you would understand if I hated you. I didn't hate you; I was confused. Now I hate you so much I swear I could hate you forever.

May 22, 2011

I know that we all change, although there are still patterns. I feel like I've lost it though. I want to find that old someone, but I don't know where to start. I feel like I've grown to become this bitter, cynical person who has thousands of excuses to hate life. Excuses, not reasons. I may have a reason or two in the past, but the past has gone. I want to find her again, but I don't know where she is or who she is . . . or who this person is. I swear this sounds cliché, and I even despise myself for saying all this.

I think that person, years ago maybe, had a lot more to bear with less whining. That person did not go out of her way for curiosity's sake. That person was certainly not weak; even her teachers told her that she was being too hard on herself. She even exercised regularly. She wrote regularly. She led a man out of his addiction for a while; now she becomes that man with the same addiction. She had trouble opening up all right, but she was happy—at least happier. She was happy with coffee, bossa nova, and a book in a crowd by herself.

Now this person, this terrible person, sees life in black and white. She looks at things without really seeing them. She is harsh on some people. One minute she's euphoric, and the next she drowns in her misery. This person is full of regrets, anger, confusion, and God knows what else. This person is a walking diagnosis. This person is the monster that the person before promised she would never become

May 23, 2011

Everything feels so empty, so meaningless. Why do we put artificial meanings on things? Self-made meaning. It makes everything like an empty glass: transparent, empty, and hollow.

I wish there were a switch to not feel a certain way or to not feel at all. How would you feel if you were to cry at everything, to space out between conversations, to feel dead when you're alive? Isn't abandoning life the saddest thing for a perfectly alive human being?

But in the end, you're alone—have always been and will always be alone. You exchange words, engage in conversations, fulfil your egos, fulfil your needs, but in the end, is there such thing as altruism? The glue that holds us together? Are we not glued by our own needs?

May 24, 2011

When was the last time you made a mistake and still considered it as a mistake that you won't ever forget?

I've made a lot of mistakes in the past, sometimes mistakes that I've never told anybody about. I was a very private person back then, until I met a few people whom I shared some of my mistakes with. Until I met them, I either blamed myself or others for what happened, but apparently, that wasn't always the case.

They gave me perspectives, other ways of looking at "mistakes." Some of the people I blamed for what happened, for instance, turned out to be doing the best they could at that time, just as I was. I wasn't always to blame either. I was only doing the best I could at that time, the best I knew how.

Sometimes, it's not a slap that we need to wake up, just a perspective. We are all doing the best we can, which includes seeing things from a certain perspective and perhaps not being able to see from another. I was told to stop being harsh on myself and/or the people around me. I'm trying, but I'm trying in the best way I know.

It's like wearing shoes that are too large for your feet: you can walk in it but it won't be comfortable. There is too much unused space. Bounded by space. Unused space. They're supposed to make you comfortable, convenient space. But no, unused space is alienation. Unused space is a wall preventing you to make use of yourself.

Unused. Unused money. Unused things. No purpose. Empty meaning. Ghosts. They're there, but they're unused. The only meaning they have is when they're used for a purpose. They're just waiting there until it's they're used again. But the forgotten ones—they're left unused, waiting to be thrown out, destroyed, recycled.

May 28, 2011

I didn't realise that the days of waking up excited are not over yet. I was shopping online—an amount I can't afford—then it says that three days ago I just bought some of the same stuff, at the same hour: eleven in the morning. No matter how late I sleep, I always wake up at ten. I also realised that I forget so many things these days. Not small things like forgetting car keys or phones, but major events. A friend was talking about stuff we did, and I couldn't remember. Same as I couldn't remember buying stuff online. Another friend told me I was just not living in the moment, but there's a possibility that I won't remember buying things I just did and I was excited about this. How can I forget something that's exciting? I would forgive myself for not remembering to bring the keys, but I forget major events. This is absurd.

I also go ballistic when people piss me off. I impulsively traded my car. I bought my previous car at the same time of the year last year. What the hell is wrong with this time of the year?

May 31, 2011

My days are empty. My relationships are empty. Everything is a matter of distance, because distance is the only thing that's real besides time. Time and distance—when combined, it's a slow and painful death. It's not a matter of geographical distance; it's the invisible distance that hurts the most. It's the invisible distance that takes up so much space, leaving everything empty. Unused space. Some days I wish to sleep and never wake up, and that would be fine, because if I leave it would still be fine. Everything would be fine.

This is not good; I just want it to stop. During the day, I sleep, and during the night, my eyes just won't shut, but I can't control it. The things that are supposed to ease aren't doing their job.

I'm both euphoric and drained. It's better to be on one of the extremes but not both . . . not both. It's as if my hands were being stretched in both directions. I have the energy to sulk, never-ending sulking. I wish I could just sleep it off, which at inappropriate times I do, but the times I wish to escape, I can't.

This is worse than being one way or the other. Plain excitement or plain melancholy, but not both. I hate to sound exaggerating. I even wish I could shut myself and stop, but I can't. It only makes the rage grow even stronger. I'm not merely complaining. People have different pain thresholds. This is draining me out. I have the energy, the impulsivity, but lack of contentment—or just simply the willingness to live. Everything just cancels each other out. Empty.

Plus, I have gone twice off meds and was unable to sleep. I am hooked on sleeping pills. I hate this.

Fate is the cruellest and kindest of all. When we blame fate for what happens, it is both cruel and kind—side by side. When someone wonderful comes into the picture out of nowhere, it's fate. When that person leaves and we run out of reason, it's fate.

"Meant." We want fate to be kind; we want fate to be cruel, to teach us a lesson. Because if there's no lesson to be gained, what can we get from a misfortune? We're never satisfied with nothingness. There has to be something. "Experience is what you get when you don't get what you want," but the word *experience* is highly disputable, relative. Are you sure the lesson learned doesn't come from our own self-defence mechanism to justify things, to merely make us feel good about what happened? To avoid not getting what we want, so we shift our want to something else: experience?

What if a misfortune is just a misfortune? What if there is no next time? What if all those lessons that we've gained to help us prepare for the next time become useless when next time never comes? What if everything is just a once-in-a-lifetime experience?

June 3, 2011

Look who's drowning now. Look who's drowning in nostalgia, where everything is artificial except time and space. But are we not bounded by time and space? Who are we if we're not entities defined by the limitation of time and space? I feel so insignificant in terms of both time and space, and at the same time, I'm in my own world of my own time and space. Isn't it strange how we're so contradictory yet we fit in the same term of the contradiction itself?

Everything is only true when compared to something else. Even what is true is something so subjective. How can we know something without comparing it to something else? Null hypotheses. How can we reject something as falsifiable if we have nothing to compare it to? Now everything seems to mean nothing, because I have no comparison. Everything seems so meaningless because I know that everything that I compare to has just the same level of meaning as I do. So it makes everything meaningless; the subjectivity of it makes it so meaningless.

It feels as if I have been trying to find meaning in empty words. Every word I have encountered has only helped me to convey what I'm trying to say, but they never attribute any meanings to every aspect of things I have experienced. Maybe some only have to feel, but I don't feel anything. I feel hollow.

June 6, 2011

All along, I thought I had been homesick, but it might not be fully true. I thought I longed for a place, but that place may just be purely hypothetical. Maybe I just long for a certain state of mind. What was wrong? I wish I could immerse in my own subconscious and just find out, I wish everything would just be that easy. Digging is tiring; revealing is hard. What would you do when you don't even know where to begin?

I feel like I have made a mistake, but I can't seem to get a grasp of what it is. I feel like something has changed and it's not necessarily for the better. Isn't it funny if you think of life as being ever so static, so still, and you feel different? But it's you; it's not life, just you. How can everything be so different yet at the same time they never really change for the better or worse?

June 7, 2011

I hate this person so much I want to drown her and strangle her with my own hands. I don't know this person, yet I have to see this person every day as she stares at me in the mirror, every day.

I just want to sleep forever and never wake up.

June 8, 2011

Talking is easy, but conveying isn't. How many empty conversations can you recall? Conversations where you would talk and talk, meaningless talk, without actually conveying anything? What if it was the other person? What if you're talking to someone and that someone has actually so much to say but you're just not giving the chance they deserve?

Every day, everybody has got so much to say—we've got so much to say, but sometimes we just don't have the capacity to deliver it. How can we have the capacity to store so much and not enough to communicate? Even sometimes words can only go so much. Everything is lost in translation; from our minds to out there.

Or maybe there are just not enough people to listen, or who want to listen. It's just sad; I am sad. I am sad to realise what an insensitive person I am, and how insensitive people can be. Maybe it's just a little too helpless, selfish, and desperate of me to hope for the world to be a little bit more sensitive. I've said before that we judge so much and learn so little. We judge people who don't fit to the societal norms without even knowing their battles. Sometimes, even if we do, we judge the battle they're going through.

Understanding, listening, being there altogether. I haven't found much lately. Everybody is talking about individuality, and everybody is embracing uniqueness. If everybody wants to be unique so much, then we have so much in common and not so many differences. We are just as small as we despise each other and as big as we admire each other. We're not that much different, you and me, are we?

June 10, 2011

I want a break from life, but at the same time, I don't want to be weak. I want to close my eyes, but at the same time, I'm scared of what I'd be missing. I want to remember, but at the same time, remembering hurts. I want to kiss goodbye, but letting go may just not be an option right now.

It's as if I have no control over my own feelings—the only right I have is taken away from me. Even my feelings are socially constructed. What am I, naked? When everything else has been stripped off?

Most of the times, I have all this excitement that doesn't seem to wear off over time, but reality is often disappointing. So I sleep it off. I sleep everything off. During the day, I sleep for a few hours because during the day I have nothing to look forward to. I'm not the kind of person who dreams much during sleep, or at least I don't remember them anyway, so it's better. It's an escape, because when I wake up, I've skipped at least a few hours. Empty hours. It's bleak. I wonder, *If I go home, will things be better?* This is why I was hooked on things, because I was able to escape. Everything I said was just a blur; time passed by so easily. I don't remember most of the things I did, though I know during those periods I hurt and lost many. So I don't know which one is worse: to be at permanent peace and end up alone or fighting it and faking all the conversations just to keep them there.

You know, it's as if I have been walking blindfolded, and when I finally open my eyes, no one's there.

June 11, 2011

So I've been thinking of an escape, but I will have to sacrifice the time I have in Jakarta. This is such a hard choice, but I haven't been able to stop thinking about it for the past couple of days . . .

Thinking of an escape helps me to stop being such an emotion ball. It's comforting to think that when it all gets too much, I can just fly out to somewhere foreign where I don't have to talk to anybody. Even if I don't carry out the plan, to know that I can is comforting enough.

You know, somewhere like Paris. I have been thinking about walking to places I've been, and it's comforting enough.

June 12, 2011

At some point of time in your life, you meet people who change your life for good. Their presence remarks a turning point in your life. I met one of them in high school; his name was Michael Kelly Reagan. He was my English teacher. Most of the kids at school didn't like him. Some even hated him so much, including some teachers, and I think it might have been one of the reasons he quit. I'm not sure why though. I thought he was pretty great. He made us read great books, some life-changing books, I suppose.

Before he left, he called me in to his office and gave me some more copies of the books he thought I should read. I asked him some personal stuff and his own views on things, like if he believed in God, fate, misfortunes, childhood, parents, growing up, adulthood, and a lot of other things. We talked about suffering a lot. I guess it was partly due to my "growing up," so times felt a little bit dark back then. He was in the Vietnam War, if my memory is still reliable. He told me about a lot of stuff, all this stuff that other teachers never bothered to talk about. I can't remember in details, but it was the kind of stuff that I still thought about even after I left his office. I thought about it at home, in class the next day, or everywhere, really. I remember him saying something about religion. "If people do something good, it should not be because they're afraid of something, including God, but because they really want to do it." Or something along that line. I also remember him talking about life after death. He said that believing in it, whether or not it exists, gives people the courage and strength to carry on. He was the sort of guy who believes in the grey area, that everything happens for a reason if you look hard enough.

He, among a few others, convinced me to stay in high school. I didn't know where I was going, but he assured me that staying would pay off. So I stayed, and I'm glad as hell I stayed. It wasn't an easy year, that very last year. But I ended up here, so I'm pretty glad.

I wish I could talk to him again though, to talk about stuff that I've discovered ever since. Maybe to ask some more questions. I don't know where he is now. I heard he moved back to the

United States, but who knows. He just left. I guess some people just do. Sometimes, when I sat on the chair in front of his desk and listened to him talking, it felt as though he was talking to me, but he was talking to himself more. Even though he was mostly answering my questions, he was also telling me about pieces of his life that he thought weren't answered.

I never really understood some of the things he said back then, but I encountered them, years later, so I've only begun to understand. So if I could, I would like a chance to talk to him again, because I have some comments to add to the conversations we had, and some more questions to ask. He planted seeds, and I must give him some credit for most of the things I'm interested in today. He planted the seed of "why?" in me to a great extent. But I guess I must be satisfied with having met him. I was lucky enough to have met and learned from him. He was a great teacher. Not just academically, because he was the kind of teacher that teaches you lessons that you would remember for life, directly or indirectly.

June 21, 2011

No matter what I feel, sad or happy, it's always there. I can't escape. It's embedded in my own shadow, following me everywhere. It's not like a headache that you can get rid of by taking a painkiller. I know what I'm missing here. But once a thing is gone, it's gone forever. So I need a replacement, not just a mere distraction. The things I thought have replaced it only distracted me and brought me into something worse. So I don't know what to do.

June 24, 2011

You wake up one day and you don't recognize the life you're living anymore. The people have changed, most of them you've driven away, and the things you love just don't exist anymore. Everything's gone. It's like coming home to a house you once called home, but the furniture isn't there. The house has a different colour now, and you're just a stranger.

June 30, 2011

I'm here, so I should be happy—that's what I've been telling myself for the past couple of days. It's still someone else's life, but this is all I've got. Mom's been telling me to go see the doc, but how can he possibly understand? How can anyone possibly understand? What am I supposed to say anyway? That all I see is a dark tunnel with no way out? Or that every day I wake up wishing I were somewhere else, though I have no idea where I'm meant to be? So I should be happy, I really should. I tried going to places I used to love, but it doesn't feel the same anymore. I don't seem to interact the same way as well. I want an escape, but I don't know where to go.

July 3, 2011

What's real? My friendships are real, although we don't really exchange much. We mostly talk about other people—you're probably one of the things other people talk about. Or we talk about how other people make us feel, the effect they have on us. We sit for hours without really saying much. We talk, but we don't say. The best and the worst things are kept hidden beyond those layers. What layers! Maybe it's insecurity, or just the feeling that they wouldn't understand anyway. I hate to think that I'm underestimating the capability of others to understand, because at times I don't even understand myself. I mean, how much do you really know about the person you're talking to? You may have known them for years, but how much do you really know? You're talking to this cheerful person who doesn't seem to have a care, who is easily amused by your lame jokes, but for all you know, after you've each gone to your own car and driven home, this person might just think about ending her life, over and over again. Or you're talking to this guy, this wonderful guy who's got tons of jokes, and again, for all you know, he might just be using his jokes to keep things under control, *his* control. So you wouldn't talk about anything else other than to laugh at his jokes. Because without his jokes, he's naked, or you never know what he's hiding behind his jokes.

So we'd sit, we'd order drinks, conversations would flow—but the flow brings nothing with it. We'd laugh you know, laughter comes easily sometimes. But maybe that's just what we need, to sit there and talk about nothing. Because the real conversation might reveal things that we don't want ourselves to hear, to know, to acknowledge. Maybe, if you were carrying out a real conversation, you'd find yourself saying things you've buried for so long and it would just leak, word by word.

So I watched the beaver last night, the one about a depressed guy who comes out of it by talking through a puppet. The puppet is him, but at the same time, it's just a medium to represent him. But that doesn't really cure—only becomes his alter ego. So I wonder if that'll work for me. Maybe having a conversation with yourself helps, with the help of a medium. Maybe it makes you feel safer to be someone else; maybe it's easier.

July 6, 2011

I asked Ahmad Fuadi during his book launching, "How can we really see, or differentiate, the thin line between being optimistic and realistic?" He said I was too young to ask that question. I published a review on his book, but he never answered my question.

July 12, 2011

What you see is not always what you get. Genuine people are so hard to find these days. Everybody is a liar unless proven otherwise. But then again, what kind of proof do you need? What kind of proof that can fulfil your expectation? Even your own expectation can deceive you. I guess time is the only thing that's real. It's the only thing I believe in.

Everything that's happened ever since I was born has taught me not to trust anyone—including myself. I thought I've always had a grip or at least a few. But maybe I myself have been wrong. I've been deceiving myself. Who knows?

Everybody leaves, which is the harsh truth. Death is the only thing that's absolute. In the end, you're alone. You always have been, always are, and always will be.

Everybody's broken; everybody's damaged. I don't care about what your damage is, and I don't want you to know about mine either. Can we just live the happy part? No one gives a shit about your shit. Everybody's got their own shit.

I wish I could care less, you know, but I guess this is just me—caring too much while at the same time trusting never comes easy for me.

Everybody's been disappointed. Some succeed to overcome their disappointment, and some are left damaged. I don't know where I stand, but I don't need you to hold my hand to keep me steady. I can stand this. I've promised myself that I can stand this. Whatever it takes, I can stand this. Because I've got no choice other than trying as hell to just . . . stand. For my own sake.

Sometimes, you gotta be selfish to survive.

But what's the value of surviving when you've got no one but yourself?

July 13, 2011

So this is the classic story: you're manic, you feel like you're on top of the world, and you stop taking your medications. Because you don't want to stop feeling that way. You don't want the euphoria to end. But nothing stays. That's something I always forget. I am euphoric now, but in the next two or three weeks, I'll be needing you to pull me out of the grave I will have dug by and for myself.

I am still a hedgehog and hence the hedgehog's dilemma.

July 16, 2011

So some ignorant doctor came to my room and told me to try to be "unipolar," saying that I should be the one to control my emotions. It's easy for him to say. He should try being me for a month. Try riding on a roller-coaster ride every fucking day. If he doesn't vomit from it, then I'll bow down. I'll follow everything he says. But until then, nobody has the right to tell me what to do or what not to do.

I don't care if I sound arrogant, if that's what I am.

July 20, 2011

I've been sitting here, people watching, for almost about two hours now. I saw a girl walking in twelve-centimetre heels. Her face looked like she was in pain. She didn't look formal . . . So maybe that's just how she would normally dress. Who knows? Then I hate the fact that I don't have my laptop or iPad with me cos typinh with this goddamn phone is just a pain in the fingers.

Two days ago, I met my ex two, whom I haven't been in touch with at all for almost six months. We talked about change, mostly. It was sad, mostly. But most of the things I wanted to say were kept in silence because that's just the part of me that I hate; when I have too much to say, I stunt and say nothing at all.

Isn't it funny how much and how little we've changed, for different parts of us, across time? I mean, in a big way, I've become the person three years ago I swore I wouldn't become, ever. In some other ways, I've achieved things I never thought

I would. So I don't know how I feel about change, really. I guess it depends at the time of the asking—when I'm the social, outgoing, and overly friendly Safira, I would say no, for a lot many reasons. If you ask the quiet, unsociable Safira who would refuse a drink, then I would say yes. I would be proud of myself.

Now this is the confusing and conflicting part. A lot of people whom I care about very deeply expect me to be either one. The problem is I can't be just either one. If I were to follow my own heart, I would still hurt the ones I love the most: my mom and myself.

July 28, 2011

Not to acknowledge the sickness and refusing to be treated is a choice and is sometimes a much easier thing to do. But the hardest part is when you're asymptomatic or oblivious to yourself of your own sickness. You refuse to believe in the eyes of others, because you look and feel good. I hope it's not too late to fix things, to reverse the damage I've caused. A much braver and harder choice is to acknowledge that you're not healthy, that you do need help—and to finally seek, listen, and receive it. I guess depending on yourself is not enough sometimes, because after all, we don't live for ourselves alone. Maybe being strong isn't about putting the world on your shoulder and believing that we are capable of doing it, but instead admitting that we are not strong enough, sometimes, and finally asking for someone who is willing to share it with you.

People, starting from acquaintances and those who are the closest to me, have said to me repeatedly over the few past months that I've changed. At first, I refused to believe the change, not only because it sounded like a negative change, but also due to the fact that none of them would elaborate the change they saw in me. The only explanation I got was that I changed to the extent that they felt like I have become a different person, a person they didn't recognize at all.

I wouldn't lie by saying I didn't see the change coming and what I'm going through, but until yesterday, thanks to one of my best friends, I refused to stop reversing things back to the way they were. Apparently, I'm in a much bigger mess than I thought, and if I keep doing what I'm doing, I'll be going down a very steep hill and nothing will be able to stop me, even myself.

Sometimes, when you cry and whine about the biggest problems in your life to a friend, what you need isn't to be comforted and to be given a pat on the back. The ones who care about you would, if necessary and applicable, give a harsh and cold slap in your face to wake you up. It will hurt, it will sting, but it's going to force you to make the change *you* want, the change you *need*. Because what you want is not always what you need—cliché, but true. To push you to start. I thought until I was thirteen I could handle things by myself, knowing that I would always have my mother, because in this world it's just me and her. But to carry it all on your shoulder by yourself, dragging yourself to survive, maybe isn't always the best thing to do. People are there for a reason. We share what we can't handle by ourselves.

Then I realise family is more than just blood-related thing. It's more than just responsibilities and concerns and the safety net when you fuck up. It's the glue that holds you together. I have been given the family I couldn't choose, and I don't regret that. But I've also chosen the family, my very *own* family, whether they're biologically related or not. But aren't we all related in some ways? Aren't we all family, then?

August 1, 2011

My doc said I should stop self-medicating myself (that means alcohol and others). So I'm starting on a new drug and stopping all of the previous ones, 'cause apparently they made me gain weight. I read some reviews on this one, and they all said it makes them feel the closest to their "normal" selves. No one really knows how hard it is to be fighting this, and everyone's been so hard on me about the "change" they see in me. But they don't know my battle. They don't know how many doctors I have been to, or been taken to unwillingly. They don't know how many pills I have to take per day and the urge not to stop taking them when I feel good. And by good, I mean hypomanic, not normal but good in a bad but good kind of sense.

I wouldn't normally be this blunt knowing and realising that people do read this based on the stats, but I'm just saying that some have been so hard on me. The ones I expected to be there left because I changed. But I thank them for being honest, or else I wouldn't have seen the change they see. Also, to remind me who's really there and who really isn't, or wouldn't. The ones I thought I could count on. Well, you've only got yourself, in the end. The times when I was battling with myself, holding back the urge not to end everything, no one knows. They would think you're being overdramatic—they did, and told me to be thankful for what I've got. I'm not thankful for this so-called "disorder," despite the life I'm living in that might actually just be ruining me as well. But I'm thankful, despite everything.

They only see the change—the change that turned me into the Safira who is more blunt, who doesn't give a shit anymore about everything, the too easygoing, the overfriendly Safira. But I think I did a lot of shit I did as compensation for what I've been feeling. But I can make a justification out of everything, so I will stop here. So all I'm saying is don't judge too fast—you don't know what kind of battle others are in.

I rarely pray, but I've been praying to whoever it is, the unseen, out of desperation, because it's beyond my control, beyond my boundaries. I'm praying to be able to get out of this vicious cycle of blame I'm in. I slept it off, but every night it comes back. So what I do now is sleep . . . a lot. And play The Sims. And forgetting to save it every time, so all I do with The Sims is spend hours to make new characters I always forgot to save.

August 3, 2011

This is why I like studying, and thus why studying somehow never ceases to make me feel better. Upon reading my tutorial, I found,

> It has taken me many years to get used to seeing myself as others see me, and also seeing myself instead of my mental picture of the character I'm playing. First of all, very few of us ever see ourselves except as we look directly at ourselves in a mirror. Thus we don't know how we look

from behind, from the side, walking, standing, moving normally through a room. It's quite a lot. Second is the fact that when you read a story you create a mental picture of each character. For the first few years this is true even reading a script. You don't see yourself because you haven't had much experience seeing yourself. Thus as you act the part, in your mind you envision your mental picture of the author's character. You go to rushes and somebody has stolen that heroic figure, and there you are—just plain old everyday you—up on the screen. It's one hell of a letdown.

Ronald Reagan in Massumi's *The Bleed.*

August 4, 2011

What am I? What have I been running away from? I guess it would be my mind, mostly. It can be a very horrible place to be. Torturous. Hence the self-medications and the even bigger problems resulting from them.

August 8, 2011

Do you know how hard it is to be *in* this, alone, and when you take the wrong step, some people are there to judge you? You also have to bear to be brought here and there like a suitcase full of paperwork, on top of already feeling like a pendulum, because your parent wants to have a second or third or fourth opinion. Of course, I also want a second opinion, but second might just be enough. You don't even know which pills to take because, God, the second doctor forbids you to take what the first one gave you and the third one thinks the second isn't taking this seriously and the first one is dumb and insists on for you to keep taking *some* of the pills. You're not even sure if you should take any *at all.* First, you've experienced discomfort, but you're not even sure which causes which, but you've read somewhere that this might cause blindness and that may cause this that may eventually lead to death and you also know that some have messed with your weight in the past. Second, you're not sure because some people think you shouldn't be taking any of those at all, because they said you could handle "it" without those pills. But you know for the better that when you were off them, you went out of control and the overwhelming feelings you felt . . . Well, they're only for you to feel and to bear—not anyone else, not for them who said that you didn't need those.

You want your life to change, but at the same time, you aren't sure if you're taking the right step towards the change you want. You're scared as hell to step into the unknown, but one thing you know for sure is you don't want to go back. You don't want to go down the rabbit hole again. You don't want to go through what you went through, and though you've had your share of fun, well, you've also had your share of pain, scars, and memories of things you wish you hadn't done. There are many arrows in front of you pointing here and there, then you thought, *Maybe I should just follow my own arrow,* but then you know you've made some terrible decisions in past regarding the same arrow so you're not sure if you're well capable of making your own arrow. But at the same time, you know you have to make a decision, a decision to change your life, because you're sick and tired of living the life you've been living. Because the life you're living isn't the same as the one you were living three or four years ago, and that's exactly why you want to change it back. You know you can't change things back to exactly the way they used to be, but you know that this isn't the direction you want your life to be heading towards. So you need to make a decision, as you always, constantly need to make a decision. But you're just so drained, so so drained from all of the mistakes you've made in the past, so drained from all of the waves and the roller-coaster rides. But you want no more of these rides, none of these waves, and no more mistakes to be made. So you need to make a decision, a different one than the ones you've made before.

Next week is my twenty-first birthday, though I'm not exactly excited about it. I know what I'm asking the universe for for my birthday . . . *if* I deserve it. A clean slate.

August 22, 2011

Your friend might just be a wolf dressed as a "friend." Well, to be honest, I am disappointed. I am surprised by how judgemental people can be, though I don't expect it coming from your own friend. "You know my name, but not my story" would be appropriate for strangers. But please, you do know my name and you know my history. You can't care less by spreading stories that are not my own? Well, no, I don't expect you to care. I just don't expect you to care *that* way.

I thought being away from Jakarta would save me from being judged. No, the wolves are everywhere. So hear this, wolf, I will still do what I do and you can talk about it for as long as you want, and the only damn I give is the pity I have from seeing you spend your time meddling in other people's business. And in case you were wondering behind my back, the only reason I was hooked on something was partly because it stopped me from thinking about people like you, and the result is to be judged for having a peace of mind in a way that doesn't suit you. Try living my life, and then you can judge however you want.

Anyway, I guess I'm tired of being angry. So nowadays, what I do is just basically sleep everything off. I sleep during the day, and I stay awake for no apparent reason during the night. But I like the night-time. Everything is so quiet and the only companion you've got is yourself. It's kind of like an escape from the everyday life without having to spend a dime and without even travelling anywhere. I like driving at night too, if it's not so cold, because I hate how cold the car seat can get and it takes a while for the heater to really give off hot air. I am lacking social interactions, but for some reason I feel content. A couple of friends asked me how come I didn't do anything for my birthday, then it made me realise that I didn't mind not doing anything. I wasn't disappointed, as I had no expectations. I was pretty happy with a piece of surprise cake. I guess after all, I'm pretty happy. When I start getting angry or sad again, I sleep it off. Now I understand why that character in Murakami's *After Dark* decides to sleep forever—because it's a perfect escape.

August 23, 2011

It's weird how I no longer miss home, how I don't miss the people I used to think about every day, and how I no longer have expectations for anything. It doesn't feel bleak, though. I mean, it's about not feeling anything in particular, but not in a way that the future seems hopeless. I wouldn't say I embrace anything that comes in the way, but I just no longer complain as much. I don't think about things as much either.

Maybe because the people I used to tell most things to, well, we grew apart.

There were periods of time when I was so detached from everything. Even my ex-boyfriend had to ask my best friend what exactly I was thinking, and she said she didn't know because I never shared that much. I don't know what happened, but something did at some point, because I started becoming so open about everything. Sometimes, I was even too blunt—and that's when I lost myself. At some point, I was so lost. Then I was so desperate to feel the same sense of security I used to feel and I started to give in to every temptation, I literally had no boundaries. I lost control—I got even more lost than I did at the start.

Do you think we need to get lost in order to find out who we really are? Or is it a never-ending journey, an ongoing process? Can you ever really state in words who you really are? What if I ask you now to describe yourself, then I ask the same questions five years, and then ten years, from now? Maybe it doesn't even take you that long to change. You never know what's gonna happen to you today, tomorrow, in a week, or in a year. You might just encounter some life-changing experience that will change you for good, or perhaps temporarily.

Say you haven't met this person in a year, and you expect that person to be the same person as the one you remember that last time you saw each other. Then you find out that this person has turned into something you never imagined to be. How come it's so easy to judge when someone else changes? How come it's so easy to get disappointed when the closest person to you changes? How come it's so easy to blame them for the change they undergo? The reason why you are surprised by the change you see in that person is because you weren't there when something happened to them. If you were, you would watch the transformation—it wouldn't catch you by surprise, and you would understand.

But you judge instead, you express your disappointment, and sometimes you even blame the person for their lack of control.

Have you ever thought that maybe, just maybe, your expression of disappointment might hurt them? Of course, it depends on what kind of change they undergo. I would most likely be disappointed if someone I knew turns into a junkie, and perhaps expressing my disappointment would stop him from going down the hill. But before you express your disappointment, have you taken the time to put your disappointment aside and listen to what happened to them?

Have you?

August 24, 2011

I remember when I was in first year and my philosophy lecturer asked us, "What is logic?" Then I went on to read my tutorial readings and found doxastic logic, modal logic, deontic, temporal, etc. Possibility, probability, if this then this . . .

Then from logic, I did my first essay in uni on the existence of God, where I was stuck in "omnipresence" and ontological proof.

Then I went on to study later-year sociology courses, where the term *socially constructed* was tossed in the air as if everything is. Well, the discipline sort of considers everything that way, but saying that would be an oversimplified way of explaining things, of course.

Then all of my psychology courses led me to believe that I myself am a system, a structure, where my "self" can be dissected and examined. That "who I am" is a product of social learning, through socialization and internalization. And perhaps I was being too simplistic, too naive, too easily excited, and too relieved that I started finding things in the past to blame for who I have become today.

Then every holiday, my beliefs were shaken to the core. All that I have believed in was stretched, until I got to the point where all of what I believed in, what I learned, what I encountered, and what I have, become regardless of those beliefs, were all unified into one big confusion. Lost.

August 26, 2011

I think I do believe in God after all. I just never referred to God as "God." I have just never given a name for it. I don't know. It's as if I simply feel strange referring to it as God because I feel like it's constructed by someone else. I also grew up with the term in Indonesian, or in Arabic, but I've associated both terms with all of the things that I learned during those years at Islamic schools. I've never quite agreed with most of the things I learned, so I feel like those terms belong to someone else. Which means if I use those to refer to my own concept of "it," I feel like "it" is a concept made by someone else, so I don't feel comfortable. I know it's all linguistic stuff; it's just I make a lot of associations, so it's kind of important for me for "it" to have no associations with religious or philosophical teachings. What I like about uni though, when I learned about the existence of God, is that they are simply questioning without providing any answers. The Islamic schools I went to, on the other hand, provided the answers for me one-sidedly. In fact, they never gave room for questions. So when I pray, I refer to "it" as you. I don't know if I considered "it" as a friend, a parent, a guru, or maybe a combination of all. I guess I just need a figure I could mentally lean on in times of desperation.

August 27, 2011

I close my eyes and imagine me standing at the top of Montparnasse, looking at all the yellow lights. And the meeting of the lights and the sky. Then the world would disappear. All of the mistakes I made, I forget about them. All of the painful things that people said are replaced by the laughs and the joy I had with the people who actually care. I close my eyes, and the world disappears. I close my eyes, and all of the memories of doing the little things I loved come to remind me that part of me still exists somewhere. I close my eyes, and that part of me who laughed a lot whispers to me that she will never leave me. That she is me, and I am her. I am a combination of all the things that have happened to me, the good and bad. She reminds me that the good memories are real, that they happened, and even if the people in there have now left, it all happened. Memories are there for a reason, to remind us how far we've come, what we've lost, what we've gained, and why we changed. Why we're here.

Nothing's ever lost. All the people I have lost, they live in my memories, and they became infinite. They don't age. They don't become older. They're still exactly how we remember. They are immortal—they're alive.

So I close my eyes and I'm standing at the top of Montparnasse, looking at the city lights of Paris. Then no one can touch me. I've travelled far from reality. No one can hurt me with words, because there are no words involved here. It's just me and the city lights. I am the silent observer. I am both the subject and the object, and I understand everything in my own sense. My own sense that needs not to be understood by anyone except me. Because I have the right to understand the world my way.

September 1, 2011

I spent most of my childhood running around or sleeping at my mom's office. I remember sleeping under her desk, which would freak out anyone who came in to her room. Sometimes, I would go to my dad's too, but I don't remember much except playing with his clock on his table. My mom said I never got angry too, rarely cried, and never really spoke a word. But I was active, doing things on my own. She said when I got upset, I wouldn't cry or say anything about it, but I would sleep instead, just like my dad. I guess I have been an avoidant my whole life—or at least I've been avoiding confrontations. Or maybe just a low tolerance to stress in general. But I notice that stress-induced sleeping is now popular among the people I know, or maybe I've just noticed. But I talk now when I get upset, I just wouldn't talk to the one I'm pissed with. Maybe it's passive aggressive. I don't know.

September 3, 2011

I would give anything not to feel this way, not to have the urge to stop feeling like this. I would give anything to stop wanting to close my eyes forever. I can't see the end of the tunnel. I would give anything to make it all picture perfect, to not to have to bear this. To not to feel so constrained by everyone's expectations I can't fulfil. It's strange how you're always told to stop pleasing everyone but yourself, but in the end when you finally decide to put yourself first, you're still not happy. Because you're not a hermit.

September 27, 2011

For those who know me well, this will be so easy to imagine.

I am on the eighteenth floor. It's a weekday, and it's around twelve or maybe two in the afternoon. I'm sitting on the sofa watching TV with Ita sleeping on my tummy. I'm wearing my light blue pyjamas. I have my blue-pink sheep blanket on, because you know the air con is always too cold even when it's set to twenty-three degrees. Then perhaps you would call me asking where I am, and I would tell you to just come because I'm too lazy to drive. You would then come and force me to take a shower just to get something to eat. You would get mad because Ita keeps trying to get close to you and you hate cats. Then we would go out for a lunch and just sit for hours, then he would come join us and we'd spend hours laughing over silly jokes we make.

Or if you were a particular person, you would just show up at the elevator because I've given you your own set of keys. Then I would hug you and sit on your lap for hours while we watch HBO. We would get hungry and then we would go out to that place we love. You would tell me not to wear any make-up and convince me that I am not fat until I finally feel less self-conscious to go.

Or if you were another particular person, I would go pick you up at your campus because it'd only take me five minutes to get there. Then we would go to that place in the old town and take hundreds of pictures, because that's just what we do. We would talk and laugh and I would order a pina colada and you would order a milkshake or an ice tea, or iced cappuccino. We would talk about the old days and how we were years ago, about our exes, and wonder what we saw in some of them and laugh at ourselves.

If you were another particular person, every holiday we would spend our parents' hard-earned money and order drinks and buy things and take them until we forget everything. You never remember anything. Because I guess that's always been the point.

Those were the times when I actually looked forward to go back home, because I had one. Now things have fallen apart and I don't even know if I can ever get myself together, even though I know I have to. This is just too depressing to think about, so maybe it's better to just sleep again and dream about happy things.

September 28, 2011

I've always wondered about my own take on some things, whether or not I should continue doing some things. But I think some decisions were made at the start of the journey. Sometimes, I decided to keep this blog private, but then, time and time again, I kept switching it back to public. I don't know why, although some comments do bother me. There has never been hatred involved in those comments. But it's always been the opposite, which is why it bothers me. A lot.

In real life, I am not who I seem to be as reflected by what I've written. It really bothers me that in real life real people actually approached me thinking like they know me just because they read this shit. This is shit. This is the shit part of my life that I write about. So don't bother showing up on my door, because I am just a different person in real life. Don't give me advice I don't ask for. Don't bother trying to save me either—you're not a hero and I am not a victim of anything. I'm just a girl who rants a lot, and after I rant, I do have a real life to continue living.

I'm torn between sharing and keeping things private. Why I share these personal things, I don't even know. Sometimes, I wonder why some people would actually read this too. I don't know why I sound angry . . . Heh, I don't mean to be. Oh, well.

September 29, 2011

Do you know why I kinda believe in it? Because when I'm off them, the sadness and the hollowness come back crawling on me. It's like they're always there, waiting, and whenever I'm off-guard, they just attack me like virus. So I go back to being on them, again and again, because they provide a shield, a protection against my own feelings. So the hell with definitions. I am done with trying to define it and helplessly trying to find a label for it. For all I know, taking them every night helps, and I am done listening to people telling me what I am and what I am not. They're not the one fighting this, I am.

October 1, 2011

Today, I am feeling content. Full, but not overwhelmed. There are no workers on the street outside, it's so quiet. But not depressing kind of quiet. No BBMs today except from my mom, so no fuss. I thought of some people and wonder how they are doing, but it didn't leave me feeling nostalgic or sad, or left out, so it's also a good thing.

The sun's been hiding for the past couple of days, so Canberra's been a little gloomy, but it's so peaceful now. This city is like a sleeping baby. I did have a headache that wouldn't go away, but when I was watching the clouds from my room, I fell asleep for a while, and then when I woke up, it's partly gone. When I was breathing some fresh air on the balcony, I felt so OK, and then I thought, *I want to feel like this moments before I die.*

October 3, 2011

I know that people have told me to be grateful, and believe me: I am, at times. I know that some have gone through far more worse than I have. I know that some people even consider it as foolish, but I just want a perfect escape, an ultimate escape, an absolute escape. But I can't stop thinking about everything that went wrong. I tried to think about happy times, but it makes everything seem even more bleak. I can't help remembering how his hands grew colder as I was holding them. I know that it wasn't my fault, but I can't help thinking about it. When I think about the people I love, it makes me even more sad, it makes me think about the times when everything was right, and I don't even any slightest hope that maybe it all could be better and good again. The fact that I have disappointed so many people in my life to the point that I've driven them away saddens me. I didn't know how to do better; I still don't. I just want this all to stop. This thinking, this feeling, all this.

October 4, 2011

I used to write stories. Short ones, mostly. I used to write a few stories about my friends that would make them cry. I didn't think they were sad stories, but apparently they were. When I was ten, I submitted a story to Bobo, and now when I read it again, I think I was born to be a liar, because that wasn't what I felt about things at all. But now I don't write about anything except for rants.

It's funny how you can imagine things that never happened, but the emotions evoked by your imagination are real. Maybe that's what gets through some people, putting one foot after the other, our coping mechanism. Maybe we are all delusional at some point. Maybe grandiosity is a compensation for feeling too insignificant for too long. Who knows?

I wonder what people think about when they're driving or when they're in the shower. I like driving because thinking becomes a safe distraction. I think I do things best when they become distractions. Sometimes, I carry out imaginary conversations when I'm in the shower—the kind of conversations I would really like to have. Mundane tasks that require automatic functioning are actually really good. They give you time to think. To be honest, I rarely think about things when I lie awake in bed at night, because that's when I have nothing to do. So I play games on iPhone until I fall asleep. So instead, I really think about things when I'm doing something mundane, like driving, grocery shopping, or taking a shower, or ironing (though the clothes I iron still look like they haven't been ironed at all). I used to live in this building when the laundry was shared. One big room filled with only washing machines and dryers, kinda like a Laundromat. It was heaven. I would sit on the table for twenty minutes until the end of the cycle, and my mind would travel far. Sometimes, I would get too sad that I needed to go back to my room, or I would feel happy that I started smiling and people would walk in and they would smile back. But I wasn't really smiling at them. I was smiling over little things I was surprised I still remembered.

You know how sometimes, if I'm not too much of a weirdo, you think of this thing that makes perfect sense but apparently makes no sense to most people? I wonder if each of us has that

kind of thing, then we have something in common—things
that we don't understand and things about us that are not
understood by others. But we shrug it off. We leave it at, "Oh,
well, OK."

October 5, 2011

They say that identities are ever changing, that assumption
of it being fixed and absolute is what turns it into a crisis of
identities. It reminds me of my interview with Goenawan
Mohammad that authenticity is a political construction. We are
socially constructed beings; our views on ourselves are always
contextual. Our identities are fluid. Even national identities are
always dependent on historical as well as social contexts and
events.

And hence, our own sense of who we are, I guess. What we are
is shaped by everything that has happened to us. Interestingly
enough, and naturally enough, perhaps, one event is always
followed by another, and it can even contradict the previous
ones. I guess it is when our beliefs are shaken to the core that
we truly dig who we really are. But then again, since it is
continually changing, perhaps we will never know who we really
are anyway. In the next five years, I may not be the same person
as who am I today.

But why are we still disappointed when the people we know
change? We know for a fact that nothing stays the same, that
change is the only constancy, but why are we still astounded
by change? Why has it always caught us by surprise? The
contradiction that time brings . . . The uncertainties that are

associated with the future can make us either anxious or excited. Do we really have the choice to feel excited about the future? I guess everything is always dependent on something else. It all goes around in circles. Definitions defined by other definitions.

Pleonasm, indeed.

October 6, 2011

If I ever have a family of my own someday, I'm scared that I might not be a good mother. I mean, every time I went to a friend's house, I always realised how different their conceptions of family compared to mine. I mean, most would sit together and eat together—at least they would have breakfast. I'm not saying that my parents didn't raise me well, but I'm just scared that I wouldn't be able to provide my kids what they deserve, what I didn't have. Maybe no one will even take me as a wife. Who knows? I'm a pretty lousy person, after all. I'm scared, or more like convinced, that my marriage will end in a divorce as well. Then I'm scared that my kid will lose a fatherly figure. I must remember that I will feed my kid breakfast, every day, and drive him/her to school, every day. Maybe I'll ever learn to cook, so we won't have to rely on domestic helpers.

Man, I don't know why I'm thinking about all this. I'm just scared of dying all of a sudden.

OK, stop. I've just been looking at some old pictures, and I realised they're still there. So I'm going back home to see the ones who have always been and will always be there.

October 7, 2011

Detached and attached. Indifferent yet sentimental. Ignorant but takes things too personal. Rude and timid. Passive aggressive. Wanting to die and wanting to live. But aren't we all living and at the same time dying? Every second you're living, you're dying. Live fast and die young or live slow and die old . . . or live fast and die old enough to tell your stories to the world. Ah, who knows? Death is always around the corner anyway. Might as well live fast.

October 23, 2011

Been too self-indulgent lately, and absent-minded too. I missed a lot of appointments. Anyway, "see friendship" is fun and sad at the same time. Did you realise it's been five years? Good times. You keep looking for the prime time of your life only to realise that it's passed. But who knows what the future might bring, right? But half of my body is still sinking, and I don't want to get out of the water just yet. This used to be a beautiful lake, then it became a pond, and now it's a swamp. You used to be swimming around with all these people, and one by one, they left. You stopped swimming, but you aren't ready to leave the water either. So you just stay there, but memories are just as good as they get—flashes of seconds that became immortal, but you don't get to relive it. They just stay there, like you, while everything shifts into the state of "in remembrance . . ." You too will stay as a memory.

I still don't get a lot of things. Maybe I never will. Maybe some things are never meant to be understood.

A friend told me that to value life and yourself, you just need to remember what you've achieved. But the thing about achievements is that they're just like obsessions. When I first got them, I was excited, but now they're just things that happened in the past. So I don't know. How do you value things? What if appreciation comes and goes, and as time passes, you can no longer appreciate some things that used to be wonderful? Maybe I just need to remember how I appreciated it, even if I can no longer do so now. Maybe it's about remembering how you felt, not how you feel. Because what felt so good leaves an empty hole, for nothing as good has come in the way to replace it.

November 2, 2011

Anyway, I can't sleep. Xanax doesn't work too. You know how when you're in bed, all these random thoughts just come out of nowhere? I thought of Prof. Xavier. Again. There are only a few people who genuinely believe in me, and he was one of them. I guess he must have been one of the reasons why I love Paris too. It's so stupid how I can get so attached to certain people even if I've only met them a few times, and some friendships I have that have been built for years . . . I'm not so attached to them.

It hurts to think of how some people who used to believe in you, who gave you the feeling that you could be anything, just no longer see you the same way anymore.

If Prof. were still alive, I bet I could just email him right now to ask him about my case study of the French national identity and its stand on secularism. He was an atheist.

Who do you live for? I saw pictures of my house back in Jakarta, apartment in Singapore, and I can't seem to relate to any of it. It feels sad to know that's where I'm going back. And to realise that I'm not going back to the way things used to be. I know this is useless, thinking like this, but sometimes you just can't help it.

What's sad is when people told you that you've changed and then they just left . . . without explanation, without giving you a chance to know *how* you've changed. So you can't fix it, but then again, maybe there are some things that do not need to be fixed.

But you change too. We were once a part of someone's life. You can try so hard to survive what's lost, but for how long? Eventually, your fingers grow tired of holding on to something. You just don't have that much energy. You're spent.

Someone blamed me for something and this isn't the first time. A number of people have told me that I'm just a spoiled brat because I refuse to deal with certain things. But it's not because I don't have any reason of doing certain things. Maybe I refuse to deal with it because, well, you just don't want them to be a part of your life. You eliminate certain things, you move on, you make mistakes, and you may not learn. But you can't blame someone for not learning. Maybe they *are* learning, in their own ways, not yours. Who are you to tell people how they should behave? Just because I seem to be apathetic, it doesn't mean I never felt guilty. You have no idea. You don't get to decide how people should be punished. Don't play God.

Somebody said to me, "You're just a spoiled brat who was pissed because no one was around, and that gives you some exclusive right to be messed up." I wish you were right. Maybe there's some truth in it, but that would be your truth. I wasn't proud of being messed up, and despite being messed up, I tried my best to balance everything. I never intended to be messed up too and to lose the people that I love. And I don't go to a fucked-up university, you know, the ones where rich people send their kids just for the sake of going to some college. I don't like Canberra, but I'm living with it. I had the chance to move somewhere else, but I figured that moving here was my choice and that's what I have to live with. And for being messed up . . . hey, I've had my share of the social consequences I have to bear with. One of my close friends talked about me behind my back, telling people that they shouldn't be friends with me because I'm messed up. Thank you for letting me know that you are not worthy of my respect.

And just because I shut you out, don't say that I'm selfish or ignorant. It simply means I don't want you in my life, because of your judgemental and self-righteous attitude. Being older doesn't mean you get to tell me how I should live my life. You don't know my past, and I'm not going to tell you, so yeah, I shut people out for a reason.

November 5, 2011

After we die, do we "reconcile" with the people who had gone before us, or do we get the "happy ending," if we didn't get one? I mean you see in the movies after someone dies they are pictured as if they are reliving their old particular memories. But what if their conception of a happy ending involves a scenario that never happened?

I was watching the truth below on TV earlier, about a group of friends stuck in the car, buried underneath the snow. Long story short, one of the guys confesses his feelings he's had for the girl for a year. And in the end, despite everything that happened, the girl asks if they get out of there alive if the guy would still be in love with her. Cheesy I know. But later on, they were found frozen to death while buried in the snow, arms wrapped around each other. I think the ending could have been a lot better though.

So they didn't get their happy endings. I wonder if there is a life after death, would they meet each other again and live a life that they could have had together, or would each continue to their own scenario, involving the same other person? But what if they picture a slightly different happy ending? So they're just using the idea of the other person and replicating it and incorporating it into their own scenario?

If that is the case, death would be lonely as hell. Because then we're just living in the illusion of a happy ending, and all the people in it are actors and we are the director. But who knows? Maybe the truth wouldn't be so important after all, as long as we are under the impression that it is real. And that it makes us happy. When we're happy, what difference does it make if it's just an illusion or whether it's because things are, in reality, going so well? I guess the difference and the similarity of being dead and alive is that people who are still in the same dimension, of being alive, do have different realities, it's just we're still influencing each other's reality. But when we're dead, we live in our own reality that is untouched by others. I don't know if that would be contentment or loneliness.

November 6, 2011

Why are we here? First, you despise others' ideas of happiness, until you've walked in their shoes, and then you realise what you've been missing out on. I don't know why we judge so much and so fast. Why so defensive?

We put on guards, but against what? Against pain? Is there really such a thing as agreeing to disagree? That we accept that we are different and that's it? Is that the noblest thing that one can ever do?

What is it to question? What's the intention of questioning in the first place? I guess I know it's all contextual, depending on what you're looking for. But I guess the silver lining is . . . despite all the different questions, the different ways of questioning it, are we all just looking for the truth? Of what? Isn't this, what we're living in, nothing but the truth? What else is there?

But I've stumbled across people who ask me questions without really looking for answers. For example, I answer them, but they keep going in circles. Sometimes, I don't even know why some people ask some particular questions. Are they trying to prove something? What point are they trying to make? Might as well just take a moment, sitting alone, and ponder all the questions yourself. I guess the best answers always come from yourself.

November 10, 2011

We're putting so much effort into trying to "be," even when you are trying to stop trying at all. So it all goes around in circles, eh, stuck in an enclosed cycle, constantly going back and forth between what is and what is not like a pendulum. Who knows if even death will be the end of our helpless attempt of trying to figure out what is and what has been. Our realities are parallel, but it is in itself a lonely reality that is only for us to understand, and we are left with no answers, only helpless and desperate justifications made for the sake of the illusion of self-fulfilment.

"Bukan maksudku mau berbagi nasib, nasib adalah kesunyian masing-masing."
-Chairil Anwar

November 11, 2011

People often put so much emphasis on being objective, that you have to be neutral, unbiased to see the big picture. But how do you find balance between looking at the big picture while at the same time trying to focus on the details? How do we negotiate our own subjectivity with others' expectations? This is just why I hate doing case studies and a thesis. On one hand, as a researcher, you have to be objective in analysing and gathering the data. But on the other hand, you have to make and prove a point, so subjectivity is needed in a sense that you need to know where you're going based on what your interests are.

So then, how do we balance everything? To a certain extent, our own subjectivity is influenced by our own openness to others' subjectivity, or in other words, it also depends on our objectivity. How do we negotiate them? We negotiate on a daily basis, agree to disagree. But sometimes it's so hard to do when it comes to certain things, you know? It doesn't even have to be someone else's opinions. It can be when what you believe in contradicts with a certain fact or reality that you encounter. When your beliefs are shaken to the core. When a child finds out that Santa doesn't exist. How do you negotiate that?

November 25, 2011

Have you ever missed something so much and it never stops, even when you think that you *have* stopped? I keep having dreams about waking up there, and I am often so disappointed every time I get off the plane to realise that I'm not really coming "home." Even my "home" has an expiration date.

November 26, 2011

Someday your heart will stop beating, and that very last beat will be the end of everything. What used to be you will be just flesh that will decay over time. Who knows where you'll be then, where you'll go, what you'll see, or what you won't see? Your faith will perhaps help you, but who knows what it's going to help you with?

December 2, 2011

I don't know how many times I've made promises to myself and then broken them. Some days you feel like sleeping all day because you know when you get out and out there, you'll just do something you'll regret. But I guess one can make a life out the things one regrets. Perhaps someday I'll regret the days I spent sleeping too.

December 19, 2011

What is death? Maybe death is a personal thing. I'd like to think that death is kind of like an achievement. You survived life. Maybe life is harder than death itself.

January 2, 2012

I like listening to stories, but yours is probably one of the few I'll never find out about. At least until now, nobody seems to be willing to tell. Maybe it's an ugly one. Who knows? Maybe they want me to remember you as you were. But no story is ever ugly; every single one is poetry. I bet yours was too. And if ugly exists, you would be crying in your grave right now, just like I've been crying for you and everything else that could have been.

January 9, 2012

There is this hole that I've been trying to fill up with anything I could find. Once it was filled with pure love, and then it was empty again. I don't know how it became empty again. Then I found other things, things that were able to fill it—only temporarily. Then Mommy said I was an embarrassment, but she said she wouldn't give up on me. She said maybe she's been fighting for all the wrong things, for all the wrong reasons. She said maybe money ruins me. There are times when I feel like giving up on me too, but the thought of someone still fighting for my own well-being makes me feel like a jerk, an ignorant, selfish bastard.

So there is this hole, maybe it is not to be filled with my own joy. Maybe my joy would come from your joy. I didn't get to see someone smile because of me, and maybe I never will. But for this one person, I shall find the right things to fill this hole that will perhaps fill hers too, if she has one like I do.

Or maybe I just need to stop trying. I feel like my whole life I've been trying so hard, even just to let go. But isn't the whole point of letting go to just "let go"? I really don't know what letting go means . . . Accepting? What if you just feel the need to let go of something but you aren't really sure what to let go of and it's holding you back like an anchor?

January 21, 2012

Right now, you're the only person I'd really talk to. The only person who gets it without any extensive use of words to explain. I perhaps wouldn't need to explain, and even if I do, I wouldn't mind explaining it to you.

But I offered you honesty and you wouldn't take it, and you said honesty was all you could offer. But even if I don't know you now and you don't either, I still want to have the same kind of convos we had years ago.

My mind is a mess again, and I don't need anyone to straighten it out. But somehow, you were always able to get into the mess I was in and just be in there with me and not talk. And that's all I ever needed.

But we both always have had one thing in common: we both are so good at hiding and escaping, but somehow you'd always find me, and I'd always find you. So come and find me now because I need you to, because I can't find you now. You're out there in some city somewhere. But we made a pact, didn't we?

January 23, 2012

It's kind of like knowing that you forgot something but you're not sure what it is that you forgot. It's an itch I will forever scratch. It's about missing something that has long been gone. Oh, God, I can't wait to get out of this city; this is just sickening. I don't know where home is. Geographically, this is it. But a lot has changed since then, and I can't even draw the line for when "then" is, and so I just don't know where I should be anymore. But then again, maybe wherever I am is where I should be, or shouldn't be, same old same old . . .

February 8, 2012

Where do you draw the line between justifying things to protect you from being hurt and seeing things the way they really are, even if it hurts? "The way they really are"—now that's bullshit. Can we ever really see the same things in the same way? Can we ever get rid of our own subjectivity and everything that has made us, to make us see things the way we do now? Can we all ever really agree on one thing? One single, universal thing?

Home is where you're supposed to feel safe—the place where you hide when the world falls upon you. Then you pray like hell that the roof will be strong enough to bear the weight of it all, that you'll be safe and sound under it, that it will not fall down and crush you to death. Because it's supposed to give you some kind of protection, I guess a sense of security for the least.

But when it all fails, when a place or at least an idea of "home" fails to give you that sense of security and the comfort you need, where are you supposed to go? What is going "back," if home is only *was* and has always been an idea, only an idea or a memory, a utopia in the past that no longer exists? But you didn't realise that it was utopia that you were living in until you are now nowhere, not belonging anywhere. But I guess that way you would never find home . . . Comparison is a bitch, and she runs faster than you. Dystopia is what you'll always find, and utopia always belongs in the past, or in the future, but never in the present.

Then when home is everywhere, do you not belong anywhere anymore? When all is lost, will you then have everything?

Paradoxes are cheeky little bastards.

February 14, 2012

I finally figured out that I'm solitary by nature, but at the same time I know so many people; so many people think they own a piece of me. They shift and move under my skin, like a parade of memories that simply won't go away. It doesn't matter where I am, or how alone—I always have such a crowded head.

—Charles de Lint

March 1, 2012

Waging wars all my life. I've fought and defeated myself, and then I stood up again and fought again like an idiot. Myself and I have a very private fight club—kind of like a schizophrenic one, like Palahniuk's.

Anyway, I haven't been loathing myself, so the doc said I was healthy and stable. Healthy and stable—whatever that means. If it means not having crying spells at the sq lounge or getting overly manic and throwing off things, I like being stable. For now. I'd really like, *love*, to think that I'm behind the steering wheel, that I control the shifting of the gears, and above all, the directions for which I am headed. I've been thinking that I am, though. And perhaps it is indeed all just make-believe. I convinced myself that I am not largely controlled by external forces. But that effing doc, who has both saved and ruined my life, said that the stable phase, where I am intact with my emotions, is always there—in-between the manic and the depressive. He said that I should be careful and that I should be prepared for whatever is coming. Now, isn't that kind of like a self-fulfilling prophecy?

Then again, and I think this has been so far my biggest question and doubt, I am not sure whether "it" is internal or external. During some phases in my life, some fucked-up phases I must admit, I accepted "it" as part of who I am, and to a certain extent what I am. But then I stopped, because I realised that I was losing control over my own life, my own will, my own emotions, my waves, and my ocean.

A psychiatric office is definitely not a place for a psychology/psychiatry student. You just basically argue and question everything he says while at the same time you know exactly that there's some truth in it.

March 11, 2012

There are days when you feel so invisible. I don't know if it's good or bad. Maybe some days you need to feel invisible, to just fade away in the background as a silent observer of the motions around you. When you're invisible, you see more of the things you don't normally see, because when you're in the picture, it all becomes distorted—like a broken mirror.

March 17, 2012

This is what it feels like: you are confused most of the times. You have the energy but lack the euphoria. Dysphoric mania. You can't sleep; you want to talk to people, but each of them is having their own lives. You can't channel the energy. You feel rage too at one point. You get so angry over trivial things that you just become angry at yourself. Then you just don't know what to do anymore. Somebody asks if you're feeling all right and it's too hard to explain—you just don't know where to start—so you say, "Fine." And now all you're left with are racing thoughts, a racing heart, and an empty, big, black hole.

March 24, 2012

As if we were connected by a single thread that is getting thinner, relationships are weird: sometimes you keep holding on to it just because. And other times you despise it, just because.

March 30, 2012

You can go travel around the world, finding bits and pieces that you love from here and there. But in the end, all you want is to be with the people you can spend time laughing with, or not laughing at all with, crying, or being silent together and not speaking a word, and there would be no awkward silence. You know, longing is a bitch. But I guess all you can do is be grateful that you've met them. We walk our paths, different paths, and they may cross once in a while. I am so glad I have met a few people who have changed my life for good. And I miss them. I want them here. Is that such a selfish act?

I think I feel fortunate enough to have been able to go places. During my travel, though, I wish they would be there with me, to see what I see and to feel what I feel. Solo journeys can be so much like self-discovery journeys, when you find *you*. But during that moment, you also painfully realise that *you* need them. You need them so much you dread being there alone. Some say solitude is bliss, but only when it's a means of escaping when everything gets so overwhelming.

Sometimes, solitude is just solitude. You can be your own best and worst companion. Fate can be both cruel and kind. They say it's all in your mind, but my mind is filled with the thought of having random conversations with them. I know that this world doesn't revolve around me—I acknowledge that fact fully. But we are social creatures after all. Cohesion is made possible by interdependence, not just in terms of the division of labour. But I guess you've made me, and I miss you.

April 1, 2012

The illusion of having something is so dangerous. An idea is more dangerous than a bullet, because it can give you both hope and despair without having the real stimulus present. You can be in love with an idea. You build yourself a kingdom with a foundation of this very idea, an idea which does not exist in real life—but from which you pick bits and pieces to help shape this idea and turn it into perfection. It is only perfect in your head.

You can be in love with an idea, so hopelessly in love. You create imaginary conversations in your head based on this very idea, an idea of a person who exists in real life but with the qualities you attach to this idea in your head. What can be more sad than being in love with an idea? In a way, you're in love with yourself. But this very idea can make you happy—happier than this real person could. With this very idea, you build another life and immerse yourself in it.

But what good is an idea? You cannot touch it; it's intangible. You cannot kiss it. You cannot hold it.

But you can, in your mind.

You see, your mind can be a dangerous prison. Not essentially that it tortures you, but it's dangerous because it's a comfortable prison. It's a safe haven. You fill this prison with everything that is lacking in your real life. A redemption. A revenge. A compensation. Everything you find in this prison is what you are lacking in real life—or perhaps something that you lost somewhere along the way that you cannot regain. Maybe we're trying to preserve an image of a person who has long been gone. You create imaginary conversations with them, and that is comforting. Some may say that no one ever really dies because their ideas live through, in some people who preserve them. The spirit never dies because it is carried on by another spirit. But they're gone. And no matter how beautiful that place in your mind is, no matter how safe it is, it's a prison. It is safe, because it guards you against the things that may hurt you. But you isolate yourself in it. You're on your own. You accompany yourself with ideas, but they're ghosts. Alone in your own kingdom.

It is a prison, a comfortable prison, made of sands and built on ideas. So fragile. The more we can control what to put in this prison, the more we are trapped.

April 3, 2012

There's something about night-time that attracts me like no other. A moment of idleness, yet its stillness has so much to convey. It triggers memories and everything that's been lost and forgotten, and suddenly, when the city is asleep, all of it bursts out of nowhere—the deepest trench, or a hole you never knew it existed, a hole filled up with things you buried for so long. There's something about night-time, the time when your walls are down and you have nothing to hide, nothing to show because the audience is asleep. All feelings are jumbled into one. The night-time carries with itself a moment of clarity in-between confusions. When you are you because you're on your own.

April 20, 2012

I was nineteen when I was first diagnosed with bipolar disorder. They said that it was just the onset, at early twenties. Then I went on medications for six months, and then I stopped. I hit rock bottom. Then I started being on it again, and I was better for almost a year. Then I hit rock bottom—lost half of my front tooth too. Then I had seizures and panic attacks and was again diagnosed for BP by another doctor. He said that I must be on medications. Then last Friday, I met my doctor again and I asked, after two years since the first diagnosis, if I was really bipolar. He said, "How am I supposed to lie to you? The symptoms are all there. Soon, you'll be really depressed again, and then manic, and you don't want that, do you? That's what medications are for, to manage symptoms. I'm sorry that it may not go away, but we can manage that." And so I was broken. Then I said, "Haven't I had enough in life? Why do I have to have this?" he answered, "I know that it's hard to come to terms with bipolar disorder with people at your age, but you have to accept this." I said, "I'm just confused. A lot of people have told me that I don't need medications. So I went on and off, and at times I was in doubt, but I don't know what to believe."

"Well, are they doctors?"

And now when I thought I've hit rock bottom, I haven't. I feel so hurt right now. I can't fathom this. God, get me out of this city. Please get me out . . .

April 22, 2012

I am lying in bed, thinking, *Where did all the things that make me happy go?* I am in Bali, far away from the things that have been making me so blue for the past week, and I should be happy. Then I remember a friend asked me a couple of days ago when the last time I felt so happy was. It didn't take me that long to think of a perfect answer, because at that time I felt perfectly happy. I answered, "Paris."

I was so out of reach, nobody could reach me. But even if they could, my hands were too cold to type. He wasn't there, and I was grateful for it. I was happy alone, and alone I was perfectly happy. I remember thinking that I was so happy I could die when I saw all the lights turned on uniformly in a second at Place de la Concorde. Paris, you will always have my unspoken passion.

April 24, 2012

I am pretty happy today.

May 2, 2012

I don't know why people can just leave, just like that, in a blink. Then I realise sometimes I do that too, that sometimes I'm the villain even when I feel like I'm the victim. Maybe we're all victims, despite being the villains as well. Because in the eyes of others, you're always the villain, not them. Because in our eyes, it's us who have been victimised—even by our own wrongdoings. Either way, we're tormented in our own ways,

ways that cannot be seen by others. All they can see is how you can just walk away like that, but we're walking away with chains on our feet, dragging them everywhere. Heavy weight that will not go away—or maybe will, over time. But those chains are invisible except to ourselves. Only we can see and feel the weight of the world on our shoulders, on our feet, in our hearts. My torment is not tangible, it cannot be seen with naked eyes, but you can't feel it. Only I can. And we all judge so much; we all condemn so much.

And it's like I'm always expecting something to happen. Sitting, wondering, and pondering—all the time. I feel excited for no reason, and then I feel doomed for no reason. Sometimes, I feel like I can't cope anymore, like life is not worth living despite all the people saying, "I love you." I love you too, but sometimes it's too hard to bear. What happens when you lose control over your own emotions? Emotions are the only things that come with you, and when you lose them, do you not feel like you're stripped off naked, standing there with no meaning and no feelings? Then what is the point of life?

Sometimes, I push people away for no reason. People can get a little bit overwhelming, but I need them to death. It's all so ambivalent. I need them so much to the point I hate myself for needing them so much. I can't stand myself sometimes. I can't stand my needs and wants and all my desires because I'm drowning in them. They're all I can think about, and how they aren't fulfilled—how my own expectations ruin me. How I am not grateful enough pushes myself to the limit too, making me hate myself even more. Because I should be this and not that, but letting go seems so hard.

But they say that wants are meaningless once you get them, like grains of sands slipping through your fingers, as F. Scott Fitzgerald would say. Then it depresses me more, when I get them, because they are no longer valuable. I think, more than often, about what the hell is wrong with the way I see things, because either way I'm always sad. I seem happy, I can laugh, and then when I'm off alone, the hollowness comes back crippling at my door, knocking, knocking, and knocking, and it won't stop knocking until I open the door. And then it sucks the life out of me, and I'm naked again.

June 2, 2012

Flashbacks—they bring despair, joy, and a reminder of what things used to be like . . . and how much you've grown out of it all. I have been reading my past entries in my diary dated from to 2007 to 2010; I stopped writing in 2011 and 2008, though. I was so naive, and I was questioning everything. I was not satisfied with my life, and I was an angry person, one who kept on complaining. I didn't know what I was going on. I was at a loss—in life, love, my academic career. Where I was.

I was also dependent on some people. But what's interesting is that I now see the same patterns. I fall in love, I get lied to, I get dependent, I fall apart, and I move on. The cycle repeats. In love, I always become too needy, and for the most part, I was angry with myself for being that. I don't know if that's a normal thing of being in a relationship or what, but I don't know how you can become a totally different person when you're in one. Relationships often reveal aspects about yourself that you never knew existed, bad or good. I didn't know I could be so giving, despite having being an egoistic, selfish, bossy only child for all my life. I didn't know, despite my ignorance, that I could care about the small things they did, and it's not out of my self-interests. I didn't know, despite having built this self-defence mechanism of not getting too attached to everything, that I could get so attached, and fall apart when the person is gone.

I think the hardest part of losing someone is losing a part of you that the person brought with them. The hardest thing about starting a new page is having to find yourself again, to find happiness in other things again. I've been relying on them for a sense of fulfilment and joy, and now I've got to look for other things that I used to love in order for me to feel happy again. Most importantly, I need to find myself again, the one who was self-sufficient and content with everything. The one who doesn't blabber and keeps things to herself.

I wasn't used to sharing things with others, but someone taught me how to open up and it was both a gift and a curse. I made more friends since then, because I started opening up to new people, including the wrong people. Harsh social consequences, I must say. But if I can't gain anything from that, I'm destined to be doomed.

But I like life now. I like the fact that I don't question as much. I've made peace with Canberra as well. I found new routines, which helps me take my mind off things. I'm starting to focus on other things now. And you coming back for a bit, I won't let it take a big part of me anymore. Having been constantly involved with people for the past year, I need to find myself again.

June 10, 2012

Self-medication is dangerous. It's dangerous not because the doctors know better—perhaps they do or perhaps they don't. It's dangerous because we delude ourselves into thinking that everything is OK again, normal again, when in fact we're not dealing with what we're supposed to be dealing, though slowly and painfully: reality. We take shortcuts instead, to get immediate relief . . . to smile again without having to wait for time to heal all wounds.

My mom is the only one who knows all the tears I've shed, all the pain I'm dealing with, and she knows all the people I've lost. Every time I get overwhelmed, she'd say, "Absorb the pain. Cry it out until there's nothing left to cry." I am often so, so tempted to take the shortcuts, and sometimes I still do, by self-medicating. But what do I find? When I'm sober again, the pain goes back. Crying spells get even worse and at times are uncontrollable. You may not know about airport lounges, but I used to have crying spells there. On airplanes too. Once, I was moved to first class because I couldn't stop crying, and I didn't know why. Blessing in disguise? Anyway, not the point.

The point is that I guess time is always the best medicine—or at least in most cases. If it doesn't stop the crying, at least it lessens the pain we feel inside. Everything subsides; it all just waves. The waves will wash everything away.

June 13, 2012

My heart is dusty. I've forgotten so much. "If only" is cruel. Hope can make us seem delusional. Who are we kidding? Even your shadow leaves you in the dark.

July 3, 2012

I ricochet between self-loathing and self-loving. Last night I asked a friend, "Why are you so angry with yourself?" I wasn't sure why. Wasn't sure why he asked either. But then he said, "Maybe it's because every time you go on a holiday, you feel like you failed to gain control over yourself."

July 11, 2012

I was self-sufficient once. I didn't need a man. Then I met you and found solace in your presence, in our talks and our walks. Ever since then, I was no longer self-sufficient. There is a part of me that keeps convincing myself that I have always had this hole that can only filled by love—that when it was gone I must find it again. I keep reminiscing what it was like to have found something I never knew I needed, and God, how I long to feel that way again. But it's difficult and has always been so. I can't quite figure it out how you just came into my life and made me realise that I was incomplete.

And now you are in my life, like a foreign tree in my well-taken-care of backyard. But there has got to be a reason why you're there, here. Maybe it is my expectation of hoping to fulfil that nostalgic longing that drifts us apart. But in-between the fights, I keep on finding strength to stay that I didn't know I still had in me.

July 5, 2012

I never expect people to fully understand *this*, or me in general, because I don't really either. But what I need for you is to stop acting like a child when I'm acting like one, to be the parent when I'm being an uncontrollable, raged teenager that I can be at times. Because I can't help it. I can't help the mania and the depression, and at times, it's draining the hell out of me too.

Sometimes, I feel like we're only OK when I'm hypomanic—because that's when I'm talkative, easily amused, and make jokes about everything. But that's only a part of me, a tip of the iceberg. When I'm on the low side, you'd leave me alone or we'd have fights. Then when I'm neutral or hypomanic you'd say you miss really talking to me (or you mean the hypomanic me?), and when I'm manic, you'd go manic too.

Then I was tired from work and got all irritated with you doing nothing for the past two months, and I have been irritable not just with you, if you noticed, but you just started acting like a child.

"At least I'm not in Canberra, cold and miserable." "Oh, you can make your own money now, wow. You can multitask now, wow."

Really? So that's why I said I couldn't do this anymore. I was there at your worst, with all your rage and mood swings and crankiness, I never said a word. I didn't say a word when you said those hurtful words, though I cried like a bitch behind your back. But I didn't do anything in your face, because I wanted to become the calm one when you weren't.

I think I've been putting up with more than I can handle.

August 1, 2012

I miss you. I don't know if I miss you as a friend or as a lover, but all in all, I guess I miss laughing with you. I miss making fun of people on the plane or just anywhere with you. I miss you. I know that you're only a BBM, away but it doesn't feel the same. I know that I said that I'm too tired to go on, but I only stopped trying because you stopped trying. If you didn't, I wouldn't. I was just waiting for you to end it, because I wouldn't.

I'm not saying this because I wanna get back together, because I don't think that we're able to do so. I don't think we're ready; I don't think we ever were. We vowed that we wouldn't wanna be in a long-distance relationship ever again, and we were in one.

At the end of our relationship, I felt like I didn't know you anymore. For a week after we broke up, I felt OK. Now everything is just . . . bursting out.

This is twenty-four hours later.

I cried last night—over our relationship, over our friendship, over you. I never realised I valued you that much. I thought you were a stranger.

But I don't know.

August 15, 2012

To be able pull out the anchor from the sea. To not drown in self-pity. To live without having expectations of what life should be like. Or maybe to just have enough of little expectations to be fulfilled day by day. To work my way out around things. To not be afraid to take chances and to lose some in order to gain some more. To know when to accept as well as when to fight. To love—to love without having some preconceptions of what love should be. To let go of all the should-haves and the should-bes. To stop holding on to things that don't exist anymore. To be able to live with memories without having them drag me down. To live with beautiful nostalgia instead of painful. To laugh genuinely instead of doing it as an attempt to conceal the truth, the ugly truth of what is felt inside. To keep running forward, not away from. To not get my judgements clouded by emotions, but to know when to trust them. To realise what matters, and who matters. To get out there and live.

—

"Do you know how long a year takes when it's going away?" Dunbar repeated to Clevinger. "This long." He snapped his fingers. "A second ago you were stepping into college with your lungs full of fresh air. Today you're an old man."

"Old?" asked Clevinger with surprise. "What are you talking about?"

"Old."

"I'm not old."

"You're inches away from death every time you go on a mission. How much older can you be at your age? A half minute before that you were stepping into high school, and an unhooked brassiere was as close as you ever hoped to get to Paradise. Only a fifth of a second before that you were a small kid with a ten-week summer vacation that lasted a hundred thousand years and still ended too soon. Zip! They go rocketing by so fast. How the hell else are you ever going to slow down?" Dunbar was almost angry when he finished.

"Well, maybe it is true," Clevinger conceded unwillingly in a subdued tone. "Maybe a long life does have to be filled with many unpleasant conditions if it's to seem long. But in that event, who wants one?"

"I do," Dunbar told him.

"Why?" Clevinger asked.

"What else is there?"

-Joseph Heller, Catch 22

—

I'm welcoming twenty-two.